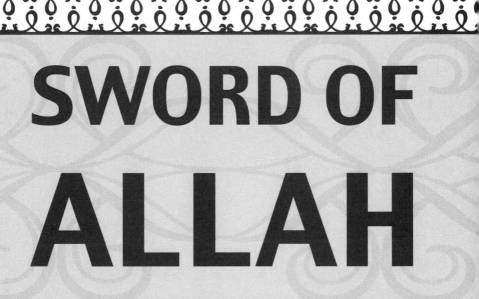

SWORD OF

ALLAH

D0109759

220.89
Zei
3/05

PO Box 1047, 129 Mobilization Dr.
Waynesboro, GA 30830 USA
(706) 554-1594
gabriel@omlit.om.org
www.gabriel-resources.com

ISBN: 1-884543-80-4

Cover design: Paul Lewis

Printed in the United States of America

SWORD OF ALLAH

Islamic Fundamentalism from
an Evangelical Perspective

David Zeidan

Waynesboro, GA, USA
www.gabriel-resources.com

CONTENTS

INTRODUCTION

What's Going On Here?

THE RELEVANCE OF ISLAMIC FUNDAMENTALISM

Following the September 11, 2001, terrorist attacks in New York and Washington, D.C., widespread public interest in Islamic "fundamentalism" quickly surfaced. Why has Islam become a breeding ground for contemporary international terrorism, and what can be expected in the years to come? For opinion-makers in the secular West, where religion has long since been eliminated from the public sector and relegated to the private sphere of free moral choices, it is difficult to understand what makes people "in this day and age" willing to kill and be killed for their religious convictions.

While most Christians have seemingly come to terms with the secular-liberal paradigm of contemporary society, fundamentalist Muslims have embarked on a process to roll back secularism, integrate faith and politics, and reinstate Islam as the dominant force in their societies and states. Their goal is to emulate the early

7

model of worldwide Muslim dominance in both politics and culture. Since Muslim decline is blamed on any deviation from the purity of original Islam, all systems not based on strict Islamic principles are considered evil, corrupt, apostate, and deserving destruction. It only follows that the use of force is seen as a legitimate and perfectly justifiable means to attain their goals.

Of course, not all Muslims are fundamentalists, and not all fundamentalists are violent radicals! According to most experts, fundamentalists only comprise about ten percent of any given Muslim society. However, their vehement discourse has had a major impact on the Muslim world because it gives voice to the deeply felt anger and grievances common to Muslims around the world. Humiliated and disheartened by seemingly universal Muslim weakness, Western hegemony, and the failure of secular ideologies (liberalism, socialism, and nationalism), many Muslims nurse an ongoing rage against the West. Conspiracy theories abound in which the "Crusading Christian West" and Judaism are the main enemies of Islam, always and everywhere bent on its destruction. As militants play to these themes by sowing poisonous seeds of hatred and distrust against all non-Muslims, they wield an influence much larger than mere numbers would suggest. One wonders at the baleful harvest these seeds will eventually produce.

For Western evangelical Christians, it is important to understand the various streams within contemporary Islam without succumbing to the prejudices, stereotypes, or "politically correct" views prevalent in Western society. In the interest of time, we will focus our attention on the doctrinal and ideological basis of Islamic fundamentalism—especially its radical forms—rather than its historical development. Primary sources written by various leaders of the movement will be used to represent its views and beliefs throughout this work. Then, by using biblical and Christian categories familiar to most of us and by making comparisons between evangelical and Islamic fundamentalist beliefs whenever possible, we will attempt to make the subject easier to understand.

The comparisons we'll be making between evangelical and Islamic fundamentalist beliefs are intended to provide understanding to evangelical readers, not to imply that both systems are valid paths to God or salvation. There are, of course, many great differences that must not be forgotten. I fully believe in the uniqueness of Christ and his gospel. However, as human beings, exploring similarities between our beliefs and experiences can help us to better understand the thoughts and behaviors of others.

WHAT "FUNDAMENTALISM" IS ALL ABOUT

The term "fundamentalism" came into vogue in the United States during the early part of the twentieth century. It was originally used to describe the revolt of conservative Protestants against the liberal stream that was taking over leadership of the churches at that time. The 1925 Scopes "monkey trial" which focused on the teaching of evolution in public schools was symptomatic of that period. Since then, the media have developed a derogatory view of fundamentalists as reactionary, unreasonable, unscientific, and obscurantist fanatics. Today, the term is typically used to describe the radical and militant movements within any religion.

In comparative religion and social studies, the hallmarks of fundamentalism are its acceptance of a divinely revealed Scripture as the complete, infallible, and ultimate authority for the believing community, and its radical commitment to apply scriptural fundamentals to all areas of the modern world, including society and state. Taken in this sense, I am not ashamed to be called a Christian fundamentalist!

Fundamentalism should not be narrowly defined but rather

'syndrome' with a large cluster of typical symptoms. ᴜᴜᴜᴜ...s have come up with a variety of lists of the main attributes of fundamentalist movements. Any movement characterized by an accepted minimum of this set of characteristics can be labeled "fundamentalist" even if it exhibits marked differences from other so-called movements or from the distorted media-inspired image of fundamentalism presented to the public.[1]

Believers who willingly label themselves as fundamentalists use the term in a narrower sense than that accepted in comparative religious studies. For instance, conservative evangelicals would be categorized as fundamentalists right along with the separatist groups who are eager to style themselves as such in the Christian world. The main characteristic of both conservative evangelicals and self-styled fundamentalists is their high view of the Bible as inerrant and authoritative, stressing the necessity of obeying its injunctions. In this sense both are fundamentalists, even though many of the separatist groups embracing the term would argue otherwise.

In a similar vein I have included as Islamic fundamentalists both "mainstream" reform movements such as the Muslim Brotherhood of Egypt and the *Jama'at-i Islami* of Pakistan in addition to the more radical and violent groups.

ISLAMIC FUNDAMENTALISM

In response to various crises in their societies, Islamic reformers began to conclude that the deviation of contemporary Islam from the alleged purity of its original form was the main cause of Muslim weakness and humiliation. They demanded a return to the Muslim source Scriptures (the Quran, seen as God's written revelation through Muhammad, and the Sunna, seen as the divinely inspired traditions of the Prophet's sayings and deeds) and to the early model of the first community, as well as a purification of Islam from later additions, traditions, and superstitions. These reformers were often lay people who attacked the monopoly of "religious establishment" specialists and worked for a reinterpretation of the Muslim Scriptures to meet the needs of the modern age.

Islamic fundamentalism (also known as Islamism or political Islam) is part of this wider reform movement, a reaction to the destructive effects of secular modernity and Western hegemony on Muslim societies. A fairly modern phenomenon, started in the 1920s with the founding of the Muslim Brotherhood in Egypt, Islamic fundamentalism aims at bringing all of society under God's sovereignty, rule, and law. Those who embrace this movement believe that the restoration of Islamic glory will be achieved by purifying society from non-Islamic teachings and practices, returning to Islam's original pure sources as the only authority, and by the establishment of an ideal Islamic state modeled on that of Muhammad and his Companions. Fundamentalists aim at Islamizing the total social and political systems of their societies and at establishing a worldwide Islamic state based on Sharia (the all-encompassing law based on the Quran and Sunna and claimed to be ordained by God for humans).[2]

Islamic fundamentalists view secularism as a rebellion against God and his law, and they see the secularist separation of religion from politics as a Western imposition foreign to the spirit of Islam. Both must be resisted at all costs. All modern societies, Muslim and otherwise, are examined in this light and found wanting, corrupted by Western secularism, materialism, and sexual permissiveness. These influences are credited with causing the modern explosion in crime and the breakdown of morality and the family. Fundamentalists condemn the passivity of traditional

Islam and challenge all true Muslims to sacrificial activism in order to roll back secularism and restore pure religion to its God-ordained position as first demonstrated during the "golden age" of Muhammad and his immediate followers.

For fundamentalists, God, represented by the Islamic system, must be at the center of the whole universe, including politics and the public arena. As a result, fundamentalism transforms religion into a political ideology that pits the have-nots of the Muslim world against an oppressive world order, demanding economic and social justice and the establishment of an Islamic state in which God's law reigns supreme. In this sense Islamism is a revolutionary ideology.

Though used as an umbrella term for a wide variety of reform movements, Islamic fundamentalism denotes certain specific characteristics as well. For example, it signals a rejection of the traditional status quo that developed over centuries and demands a radical reinterpretation of religion, both in doctrine and practice. Fundamentalists also demand a change of society, culture, and political structures in line with their interpretation of Muslim scriptures. The main division among fundamentalists is between the majority mainline groups that strive to attain their goals within the legal framework of their various states (rejecting the use of violence) and the radical extremists who use religious arguments to promote violence against state and society as a legitimate and necessary means to attain their goals. The division between the two groups became blurred when the Soviets invaded Afghanistan and fundamentalists of all backgrounds and convictions were thrown together in their fight against a common enemy. The resulting cross-fertilization brought about a radicalization of the more moderate factions.

Fundamentalists see the state as the main instrument for implementing a God-pleasing society under Sharia, and so they concentrate their efforts on capturing the state and its centers of power—either legally within the democratic framework, or violently by revolution or *coup d'etat*.

While all fundamentalists maintain a holistic view of Islam as an integrated system embracing all of life—with an Islamic state under Sharia representing the perfect implementation of God's will on earth—radicals have reinterpreted traditional Islamic concepts to justify their use of indiscriminate violence. God's unity (*tawhid*) is understood in a monolithic sense implying the imposition of religious law on the universe and in society: One God, One Faith, One Law. God's sovereignty and rule mean that no other authority can be recognized, thus all legal systems must be based on God's revealed law (Sharia). Any society not accepting Sharia is declared illegitimate and becomes the target of indiscriminate, revolutionary violence aimed at replacing it with a Sharia system.

Since most Muslim societies and states are seen as having reverted to the paganism of pre-Islamic times (*jahiliyya*), radicals feel obliged to examine and judge governments, institutions, and individuals, declaring them apostate and non-Muslim because they do not live by God's rules. Holy War (*jihad*), which in traditional Islam was waged mainly against non-Muslims, is thus being justified against fellow Muslims who do not accept radical views on religion and state. These Muslims are seen as deserving the death penalty for apostasy, thereby justifying the assassination of rulers and other public figures deemed non-Muslim. This is what lies behind the terrorist efforts aimed at destabilizing regimes in Muslim states. Such regimes are seen as enemies of God, and taking power by force is considered necessary to impose the Islamic system on the populations of those states.

While most Muslims in the West aim at integration within their host societies and enjoy the democratic freedoms and economic opportunities offered them, Islamic fundamentalists press for more.

Typically, they demand state recognition of their status as a separate religious community with the right to conduct its own internal religious, educational, and family affairs by Sharia law, and they aggressively encourage other Muslims to do the same. They claim that Muslims cannot truly follow all the precepts of their religion in a secular society, and they see the constitution of a separate, state-recognized community as an important step toward the Islamizing of their host states. The radicals take it one step further by promoting *jihad* as the God-ordained method of eliminating enemies and spreading the dominance of Islam. Terrorism against unbelieving regimes is part of the campaign for bringing all political power into Muslim hands and setting up a one-world Islamic state.

It is important to realize that, contrary to the many mollifying statements issued by Western leaders following the September 11 terrorist attacks, Islamic fundamentalism is neither an aberration of some peaceful, true Islam, nor a marginalized fringe group of lunatic Muslims who are not "true Muslims" at all, but an integral part of contemporary Islam with deep roots in Islamic history and theology. Fundamentalists simply select and prioritize different Muslim texts and historical elements than traditional or modernist Muslims.

WHY MUSLIMS ARE SO ANGRY[3]

While Islamic fundamentalists form only a minority of Muslim societies, the grievances that gave birth to the movement are widespread among Muslims in general. Though most oppose the use of violence and terror, they readily accept the anti-Western, especially anti-American attitude, that fuels these attacks. The following reasons Muslims give for their aversion to the West may not all be objectively true, but it is important to see the grain of truth within each and to understand them as Muslim perceptions of the situation. As such they are due careful examination.

1. Western Imperialism and Dominance

While Muslim states were dominant in world politics for a thousand years following the founding of Islam, Muslim countries have, in the last three hundred years, been on the defensive against an expanding West. By the end of the First World War, almost all Muslim countries were under foreign (Western-Christian) rule. Western colonial masters imposed arbitrary borders, Western systems of law and education, and secularism. While some Muslims initially admired Western power and culture, attempts at copying Western liberalism, nationalism, socialism, and capitalism had all failed by the 1970s.

2. Western Secularism

The Western concept of secularism—the separation of religion from politics and the relegation of religion to the private sphere— is totally foreign to Muslims who view it as a Western import forced on Muslim states against their will. Most Muslims believe that religion has an important role to play in the public sphere and secularism is viewed as a Western rebellion against God and His law.

3. Resentment of the United States

Muslims see the United States as heir to European political power and the recognized leader of the Western world. While it has not colonized Muslim lands, the United States seems intent on maintaining Western dominance through neo-colonial means such as dependency, economic superiority, globalization, and cultural influence. It is also accused of forcing Third World governments to implement International Monetary Fund and World Bank policies that worsen the lot of the poor and of supporting repressive regimes in Muslim countries in order to secure vital oil supplies from the Middle East. Finally, the United States is viewed as the main source of modern immoral culture, including sexual permissiveness and pornography, which lies behind the breakdown of the family and the erosion of traditional values in societies all over the world. This exported culture is seen as corrupting young people, leading to drug abuse, and fostering an explosion in crime all over the world. America has thus become the great enemy of the Muslim World, the great Satan, and the incarnation of all things evil.

4. Western Support for Israel

Following the holocaust, many Westerners became sympathetic to the Jews and to the state of Israel. While many Christians see the in-gathering of Jews to their ancient land as the fulfillment of biblical prophecies, most Muslims see Israel as a creation of Western imperialism aimed at dividing and weakening the Arab World and perpetuating Western dominance in the Middle East. In addition, they hold Israel responsible for the great suffering of the Palestinian people. Western—and especially American—support of Israel is therefore deeply resented as unjust and one-sided.

CONCLUSION

These perceptions provoke feelings of great humiliation in Muslims, especially as they compare their present weakness with their past glories. In cultures where honor and shame are important motivators to action, the shame of dependency and weakness arouses profound resentment, hate, and anger. These feelings lead to a pervasive worldview, fueled by conspiracy theories, that holds others (especially Israel and the Christian West) responsible for Muslim weakness and failures.

I

Useful Paradigms

UNDERSTANDING ISLAMIC
FUNDAMENTALISM

INTRODUCTION

It is very difficult for modern secular Westerners to understand what is happening in the Muslim world today. For most opinion makers in the West, religion is irrelevant, relegated to an individual's private life and not to be discussed in public. Very few in today's Western societies are willing to fight for religious causes, nor can they understand how people in this post-modern age can be motivated to kill and be killed for religious convictions. Since those who have not spent significant time in other cultures tend to perceive Western cultural contexts as universal, they simply assume all nations and societies value and practice the same post-modern, secular principles they do. Liberal democracy, pluralistic multi-ethnic societies, gender equality, and free individual choice seem as natural to the secular Westerner as gravity and clean drinking water. This is why we must look for comparisons between our own realities and those of contemporary Muslims in order to fully understand what lies behind the actions and attitudes filling today's headlines.

THE REFORMATION PARADIGM[4]

For evangelicals, a very useful tool to help in understanding Islamic fundamentalism and the situation of Muslims around the world is an examination of the Christian Reformation in Europe. The spiritual and intellectual upheavals in the Muslim world are strikingly reminiscent of what happened in Europe during the sixteenth and seventeenth centuries. For over a thousand years prior, Europeans had lived in a world united by the Christian church. This provided a common set of beliefs, a common standard of behavior, and a common sense of identity. Religious unity was seen as indispensable to public order and was enforced by civil authorities. To be a citizen was to be a Christian, and heretics were excommunicated and persecuted.

During the Reformation era, social unrest and innovations in mass media (the printing press) combined to create large movements critical of the corruption found in both church and society and demanding reform of religion and state. Religious belief became a matter of individual choice rather than an accepted part of birth into a community. As a result, the religious establishment lost its monopoly on doctrine and practice, laymen contributed to religious discourse, and radical social and political changes were initiated.

Two of the primary Reformation doctrines were the sole authority of Scripture and the priesthood of all believers.

Empowered by these new doctrines, Reformers attacked unscriptural customs and superstitions such as the veneration of saints and images, the mediatory powers of Mary and the saints, the privileged position of the priests, and many more. Nor did they limit their attacks to theological issues. There were widespread social and political connotations as well. Luther encouraged the princes to cruelly suppress peasant rebellions. Calvin founded a religious state in Geneva which enforced piety on all its citizens. Knox fought the legitimate Queen of Scotland. The Puritans forbade theater and public amusements in England. Radical Anabaptists set up a millennial kingdom in Munster, Germany. Kings, nobles, and politicians all took turns manipulating religion to enhance their political ambitions. Persecution of religious dissidents and long religious wars plagued Europe for a long, long time. In fact, violence became so widespread that some historians claim that up to a third of the European population was killed during the religious wars of that period.[5]

Indeed, the tragic part of the Reformation was the incessant violence that accompanied it. In the end, it was society's weariness with religious warfare that encouraged the development of the Enlightenment, secularism, and nationalism in Europe. These were seen as means of depriving religion and religious institutions of the privilege of using force to maintain public order and preserve the peace.

The overarching significance of the Reformation has not been lost on the leaders of Muslim fundamentalism. A number of them have consciously and intentionally demanded a Reformation in Islam similar to that of Christian Europe. They understood the Reformation as having released a great surge of energy that enabled Europe to jump ahead in the areas of science, technology, economic wealth, and political power, leaving the Muslim world far behind. In their quest for the secret of political power, they have tried to emulate the Christian Reformation in a Muslim context. Jamal al-Din al-Afghani, one of the initiators of modern Islamic reform, declared that Islam needs its own Martin Luther in order to liberate it from the dead hand of scholars.[6] Ali Shariati, the ideologue of the Iranian Revolution, claimed that contemporary Muslims were at an historical stage of development similar to that of Europe in the fourteenth century, which, after stagnating for over a millennium in the Middle Ages, experienced the Protestant Reformation that generated its leap forward into modernity.[7] He saw the Reformation as a social revolution that created a paradigm shift in society, releasing vast energies and mobilizing the masses into activist movements of change. So, too, he insisted that contemporary Muslim societies need a similar religious Reformation that will shift them from passive fatalism to a dynamic application of ideology to their problems.

> What is important to us now are Luther's and Calvin's works, since they transformed the Catholic ethics to a moving and creative force.[8]

> This Islamic Reformation will unleash great energies and lead to "a great leap forward" that will skip centuries, helping Islamic societies reach the level of Western societies in this generation.[9]

Muslims today are actually experiencing a similar ferment to that of Europe during the Reformation era. The crises caused by the legacy of colonialism, the population explosion, and the overwhelming pace of change in industrialization and urbanization, coupled with modern advances in mass media and the Internet have created a widespread demand for religious, social, and political reform. Long established traditions are being discarded, and there is a call to return to the sources and fundamentals of the faith.

This return to the original Scriptures and to the early model of the first Islamic community has given rise to ideas long deemed heretical by orthodox traditionalists. In fact, traditional Islam had developed partly *in response* to these very concepts because they caused rebellion and bloodshed in the past. The breaking of old taboos has given modern Muslims access to ideas that had long ago been anathematized as divisive and dangerous.

Many Muslims accuse their religious establishment of being puppets of oppressive regimes. Lay leaders arise claiming the right to interpret the Scriptures for themselves, and demands for social justice and greater economic and political equality are being raised. New movements and groups are founded and divided, giving birth to ever-newer groups. Doctrines and means are discussed, and people are fired by a fanatical zeal for their own interpretation of Scriptures and are willing to kill and be killed to uphold their utopian visions of the God-pleasing society and its political framework.

Though theology and politics are as cleverly intertwined as they were during the Reformation, it is important to note that for Islamic fundamentalists, doctrines and their interpretations are of first importance. They are a primarily God-centered movement and seek to obey what they perceive to be God's revelation in Muslim Scriptures. This is usually accomplished by tearing down worthless traditions and superstitions and rebuilding society according to the blueprint found in the Quran, in Muhammad's example, and in early Muslim history—the "golden age" of Islam.

ANOTHER PARADIGM—PROTESTANT FUNDAMENTALISM

Another useful period in Christian history that helps clarify some aspects of Islamic fundamentalism is the early part of the twentieth century in the United States. During that era modernist liberal theology effectively penetrated the establishment structures of numerous mainline Protestant denominations. After a period of struggle for control of the churches and their institutions, many conservatives (now termed fundamentalists) decided to separate from liberal-controlled churches and set up their own churches and institutions that would remain true to the Bible and its message. Following a period of consolidation in isolation, most of these fundamentalists have since mobilized to impact society and influence politics.

Islamic fundamentalists go through similar processes as they seek to separate from corrupt regimes, societies, and institutions, set up their own "pure" mosques and institutions, and then return when strong enough to reconquer society and state. This is often explained as following Muhammad's example of migrating from Mecca to Medina, setting up an alternative society that gradually gained power, and later returning to Mecca to conquer and take over religious and political control.

SOME SIMILARITIES ON A BROADER SCALE

On a linear spectrum of religions prioritized according to their closeness to the biblical revelation, Islam as a monotheistic and prophetic faith would come just after the various forms of Christianity and of Judaism, and long before Hinduism, Buddhism, and other polytheistic and animistic religions. As a result, it is not hard to identify similarities between Christian evangelicalism and Islamic fundamentalism. For example:

Secularism

Both stand opposed to modernist-secularist attacks on religion and to the secularist attempts at marginalizing religion.[10] Both see secularism as their main enemy—godless and atheistic influences enforcing anti-God legislation under the pretense of the separation of church and state, committed to the removal of religion from the public arena, and working toward its ultimate destruction.[11]

Revelation vs. Reason

Both reject modernism's acceptance of reason rather than revelation as the source of all knowledge. They similarly reject its attempt to monopolize science, its suppression of the supernatural, and its relativism in ethics and morality. Both see a clear causal relationship between secularism and the moral crisis in contemporary societies, and both are supernaturalist in theology and absolutist in ethics.[12]

Nonconformity

Both Islamic and Christian fundamentalists consciously take unpopular "scandalous" positions, refusing to conform to current fads. Both argue that "true" believers are a minority in their societies, simultaneously asserting that a large proportion of the population—the silent majority—agrees with their worldview and would happily consent to a fundamentalist take-over of political power.[13]

Marginalization

Both movements emerged partly as a reaction to the overwhelming pace of change in modernization, secularization, industrialization, urbanization, and development. These sweeping changes led to feelings of powerlessness, fragmentation, humiliation, despair, an existential loss of identity, and a deep disillusionment with the political and religious *status quo*. In all societies it is common for those marginalized, impoverished, or alienated by the inability of their respective political systems to solve their basic problems to respond with a deep-seated sense of grievance that may express itself in religious forms.[14]

Political Activism

Both movements have developed political awareness and activist political programs that enable them to exert pressure on political systems. Previously passive groups have been mobilized to assert their worldview and to make their voices heard above the dominant, secularist-elitist discourse.[15] Both are active in strengthening the role of religion in political life and in encouraging society and its institutions to accept public expressions of religion.

Inerrant Scriptures

Both stress not only the inerrancy of their respective Scriptures coupled to a literalist interpretation but from them draw radical conclusions that they seek to implement in the modern world.[16] Such similarities are the result of both camps belonging to monotheistic religions based on Holy Scriptures.

God's Sovereignty

Both movements aim at bringing their societies under God's sovereignty and law, as outlined in their respective Scriptures. Both judge their respective societies as neo-pagan and immoral. Both reject secularism and liberal theologies, calling instead for a holistic, integrative worldview and for socio-political and legal systems based on absolute scriptural values.[17]

"Narrow-minded"

Both movements are seen by their opponents as intolerant, extremist, fanatic, rigid, literalist, narrow-minded, reactionary, and obscurantist.[18] Governments, media, and the man in the street all seem frightened and confused by the fundamentalist phenomenon, not knowing how to relate to it. Liberal observers view fundamentalisms as extremist, militant, intolerant, and repressive alternatives to liberal humanism that want to impose an absolutist system on society.[19]

Religion as Central

Both movements use religion as a political ideology, claiming it should control not only personal morality and worship but also all areas of life including politics. Even knowledge itself must be "religionized" (as in the Creationism dispute) to purify it from secular atheism. Both present their programs as the panacea to all evils of society that will usher in utopia.[20]

Missionary Zeal

Both Islam and Christianity are world missionary religions that have propagated themselves successfully across the globe.[21] Their fundamentalisms are especially zealous in missions — the great number of conversions to fundamentalist (evangelical) versions of Christianity and Islam suggests resemblances in outreach methods and appeal.[22]

Back to the Basics

Both appeal to literate people with modern technical education who desire to be "true" Christians or Muslims, rediscovering the pure faith revealed in their Scriptures and practiced by the first generation of believers. Defending their faith against vicious secularist attacks, both respond by selecting a number of endangered doctrines to serve as rallying points and identity markers.[23]

SOME CLEAR AND DISTINCT DIFFERENCES

There are also obvious differences between evangelical Christians and Islamic fundamentalists as each movement emphasizes certain distinctives of its own tradition.

Inerrancy as a Doctrine

One difference relates to the processes of revelation and inspiration of Scripture. Muslim views cannot be easily compared to the evangelical view as most Muslims do not isolate the Quran from the Sunna.[21] The Muslim view is actually nearer to Catholic and Orthodox conservative views that add church tradition as an authoritative source alongside Scripture. Another difference is that the inerrancy of the Quran is not an exclusivist, fundamentalist doctrine, as in Christianity, but is unquestionably accepted as a basic premise by most Muslims.

A Product of Society

Another difference relates to the fact that modernism and secularism developed gradually within Western culture, whereas, in most Islamic cultures they penetrated from without and were imposed by ruling elites in an effort to modernize their countries on a Western model.[25] Islamic fundamentalists view modernism as a culturally alien force that has caused a serious break in the cultural continuity of their societies. Evangelicals, on the other hand, accept certain aspects of modernity, including some separation of church and state and the fact of secular governments, as legitimate.

Islamic fundamentalism developed in opposition to

imperialism, and it uses the discourse of radical, Third World liberation movements.[26] Western evangelicalism, on the other hand, is the product of post-imperialist society and shares many of the assumptions that underlie post-colonialism, including the view of Islam as the main ideological enemy.[27]

Patriotic . . .

Evangelicals tend to be patriotic citizens of their nation-states while Islamic fundamentalists tend to be pan-Islamic and consciously reject nationalism as a foreign ideology designed to divide the universal Muslim community. Fundamentalist Islamic groups support national liberation movements merely as a step towards the ultimate goal of pan-Islamic unity.[28] While many Islamic fundamentalists actively try to penetrate the political systems of other Islamic countries in the name of one worldwide Muslim nation (*umma*), most Christian fundamentalists, in spite of the doctrine of the one universal church and extensive missionary work carried out across national borders, do not have an ideological goal of penetrating the political fabric of other countries or of setting up one universal Christian state.[29]

But Not Political

Another difference is that Islamic fundamentalism is inherently more political than the Christian variety. It rejects all boundaries between church and state and posits Sharia as binding in all areas including personal status, economics, and politics. Evangelicals, on the other hand, interpret the sayings of Jesus: "Then give to Caesar what is Caesar's and to God what is God's"[30] and "My Kingdom is not of this world" as meaning the acceptance of at least some form of separation between church and state.[31]

Holy War and Martyrdom

Very important differences relate to attitudes toward Holy War and martyrdom. Islamic fundamentalism has popularized *jihad* as an effective weapon against all enemies in its struggle for an Islamic state, turning it into a terrorist ideology. Some, like Faraj of *Islamic Jihad,* turn it into a sixth pillar of Islam—the missing or forgotten obligation. Martyrdom is actively encouraged and glorified and suicide attacks justified. In modern evangelicalism, passive martyrdom is seen only as a last resort, and Holy War (Crusade) is understood only in its spiritual and symbolic sense.[32]

Self-Righteousness

While many Christian churches and institutions have in recent decades expressed their repentance and contrition for the many wrongs committed in Christian history against Jews, Muslims, Third World countries, aboriginal peoples, and many others, most Muslims and Muslim institutions still adhere to a self-righteous view of their own community and history. They find no fault in their own ranks and blame all evils of the world on others external to it. This posture gives rise to conspiracy theories, hostility, desire for revenge, and, among the extreme fundamentalists, indiscriminate violence and bloodshed against all perceived enemies.

A Religion of Law

Islam and its fundamentalist version, like rabbinical Judaism, is primarily a religion of law: a complex legal system derived from its source texts through interpretation, commentary, and case law over many centuries, yet given divine status in its entirety. This system regulates every aspect of human life in a rather inflexible form in spite of mechanisms like *ijtihad* (the right of every pious Muslim to personally interpret the Muslim scriptures) to ensure change and adaptability. True Christianity, on the other hand, is guided by the principles of revelation, especially as laid down by Christ and the apostles, but has the freedom of a flexible adaptation to changing contexts.

Meeting Muhammad

Finally, Islamic fundamentalists demand a return to the origins of Islam, hoping to purify the faith and achieve a great leap forward similar to that of the Protestant nations of northern Europe following the Reformation. Their problem however lies in the content of the original sources themselves. When Christians in the Reformation turned to the sources of Christianity, they met God expressing his love through Christ's incarnation and atoning death on the cross. When Muslims return to the sources of Islam, they meet Muhammad in Medina setting up a political system bent on expansion and world dominion, fighting his enemies, and dealing severely with opponents of his political and spiritual authority.

CONCLUSION

While it is easy to see similarities between Christian evangelicals and Islamic fundamentalists and between certain historical and social contexts (such as the Reformation period and contemporary Islam), the real issue is what the reformers of each religion find when they return to their original sources. It is the presumed revelation that is crucial, and the big difference is that when Christians turn back to the Bible they find the words and example of Christ, while Muslims who return to their source texts find the words and example of Muhammad. The basic differences then between the two reform movements are to be found in the personalities, teachings, and characters of their founders.

2

Reform and Revival Around the Muslim World

A BRIEF HISTORY OF ISLAMIC FUNDAMENTALISM

INTRODUCTION

Islam is a world religion with over 1.2 billion adherents on all continents. It is thus difficult to generalize about Islam and Muslims, just as it is difficult to make general statements that are true of all who call themselves Christians in the world today. Terms like Christianity and Islam encompass so much complexity and variety that one must carefully define which part of the whole one is dealing with in a particular context.

As in Christianity, there are many divisions within Islam. The main division is that between Sunnis and Shias. The Sunnis, who recognize the first four Muslim rulers following Muhammad's death (Caliphs) as Muhammad's legitimate heirs, are the majority group comprising some eighty-five percent of all Muslims worldwide. The Shias recognize only 'Ali (the fourth Caliph) and his lineal male heirs (the Imams) as legitimate rulers of all Muslims. Within each main group there are further sub-divisions, including those representing the legalistic and the mystical (Sufi) aspects of Islam, as well as the modern developments of liberalism and secularism.

Though each Muslim group is convinced it is the true expositor of the faith, the larger groups generally accept the main streams of Islam as orthodox and only think of the various fringe movements as heretical.

ISLAMIC REFORM

Reform and revivals have been part of Islamic history since its earliest days with reformers calling for a return to the fundamentals of Islam as expressed in the Quran and Sunna and to the original ideal state model of Muhammad in Medina. Revivalists argued that the cause of political, military, and economic weakness was the departure from true Islam. They demanded rigid conformity of individual and communal lives to the standards of Sharia and asserted that every pious Muslim has the right to personally interpret the Muslim Scriptures (*ijtihad*). Revivals were often led by charismatic figures that assumed the roles of a renewer of the faith or of the messianic savior described in Muslim traditions.[33] Though unique to time and place, these revivals also shared a number of key themes:

1. A call-back to revealed Scripture (Quran and Sunna) as the only final authority for all of life

2. A return to the ideal model of the early community (the golden age), including a strict moral lifestyle

and the reinstatement of the social and political institutions of early Islam

3. An acceptance of the usefulness of later traditions and interpretations while rejecting their authority

4. A rejection of the superstitions and pagan practices that had crept into Islam (folk Islam), including accepting saints as mediators, venerating saints' tombs, witchcraft and magic, and many more

5. A disregard for the monopoly of religious experts who demand lay Muslims follow their rulings rather than go back to the original sources (*taqlid*—blind imitation in legal interpretation, often of the leaders of the legal schools in Islam or of famous later commentators and jurists)

6. A demand for the individual right of interpretation (*ijtihad*), which had been suppressed in traditional Islam since the tenth century AD.

Islamic fundamentalism arose out of the reform movements that, since the seventeenth century, have gone through three major phases: Renewal (*tajdid*), Return to Pious Forbears (*salafiyya*), and Awakening (*sahwa*).[34] The term has currently become an umbrella descriptor for the many movements committed to the Islamization of the social and political systems of their societies, states, the Muslim world, and ultimately the whole world. Their goal is the re-establishment of a revived "true" Islam based on the "golden age" paradigm of the first Islamic state and its implementation in all areas of life.[35] Though a modern phenomenon that interacts with modern society, Islamic fundamentalism is rooted in the traditions of recurring cycles of reform that provide it with genuine Islamic symbols.[36]

THE FIRST STAGE—PRE-MODERN REVIVALS (SIXTEENTH THROUGH EARLY EIGHTEENTH CENTURIES)

As Muslim states came under pressure from Western imperialism, revival movements arose to resist the foreign invaders. They recognized the cultural, religious, political, and economic decline of Muslim societies and believed that the cause of Islam's weakness was its departure from the original model of the Prophet and the first Muslim community. This departure, they felt, had led to all non-Islamic innovations, superstitions, and practices. The more noteworthy of these revivals included:

India—Shah Wali-Allah of Delhi

Shah Wali-Allah of Delhi (1702–1762) was a Sufi reformer in the Mughal Empire's period of decline who called for a return to original Islam in an attempt to rediscover its forgotten fundamentals as preserved in the Quran and Sunna. He condemned the blind imitation of traditional teachers and reinstated the right of the individual to interpret Scripture. His vision was a new integration of Islamic law, mysticism, and theology into a powerful whole.

Arabia—'Abd al-Wahhab

Muhammad ibn 'Abd al-Wahhab (1703–1792) founded a puritanical and militant reform movement based on a strict and literalist interpretation of Muslim sources. He ensured its survival by an alliance with the tribal leader of the house of Saud. He judged the Islam of his time to be a degenerate version of true Islam corrupted by blind imitation of clerics, the Shia elevation of Imams to the role of mediators, and popular folk religious practices of the Sufi*s* such as saint-worship and tomb visitation, which he condemned as idolatry. He compared the Arabian society of his time to the pagan pre-Islamic period of ignorance and declared Muslim opponents to be non-Muslims or apostates, thus justifying Holy War (*jihad*) against them.

Sufi-led Resistance Movements

Sufi-led movements of renewal calling for *jihad* against foreign powers and for the purification of Islam emerged in areas such as Sudan (*Mahdism,* 1882–1898) and Libya (*Sanussiyya,* 1837–1931) where they founded independent Muslim states based on Sharia. These were successful for a while until dismantled by superior British and Italian forces. Similar movements also emerged in North Africa ('Abd al-Qader, 1808–1883) against the French, in the Caucasus (Shamil, 1796–1871) against the Russians, and in Sub-Saharan Africa (Usman dan Fodio and Umar Tal).[37]

THE SECOND STAGE—REFORMISM AND *SALAFIYYA* (NINETEENTH AND EARLY TWENTIETH CENTURIES)

Sir Ahmad Khan (1817–1898) in India, Jamal al-Din al-Afghani (1839–1897), and Muhammad Abduh (1849–1905) in the Middle East initiated the modern reform movement. This movement, in turn, gave birth to the *Salafiyya* movement founded by Rashid Rida (1865–1935), which led to contemporary fundamentalism. The core of *Salafiyya* is the call for a return to the practices of Muhammad and the first generation of Muslims (the *salaf*).

The reformers offered an alternative to westernized secularism and to conservative traditionalism by combining Islamic and modern concepts. They instilled in Muslims a pride in their past glory and revived their confidence and their shattered sense of identity. In addition to the older reformers' insights and demands, they stressed the compatibility of revelation with reason and science and the adaptability of Islam to the modern world. They distinguished between the unchanging core of Islamic worship and the changeable precepts of social life.

Jamal al-Din al-Afghani

Al-Afghani was a political activist who aroused Muslims to resist imperialism, revive their lost glory, and liberate their states from colonial rule. He encouraged a sense of worldwide Muslim unity, a reform of the decadent and superstitious elements in Islam, and the utilization of Western science and philosophy. He taught that Islam is a dynamic and progressive religion of reason and science capable of responding to modern contexts.

Muhammad 'Abduh

'Abduh, who was rector of al-Azhar in Cairo and chief Sharia judge (*mufti*) of Egypt, wanted to reform society by discovering the intent of Islam's basic principles and implementing them in a flexible way suitable to modern contexts. He accused the religious experts of being unable to distinguish between the unchanging core of Islam pertaining to worship and its external layer dealing with social matters that was open to change. He stressed the unity of God (*tawhid*) as the foundation of Islam's integrated worldview, saw no conflict between Islam and modernity, and claimed that revelation and reason were not contradictory but complementary concepts. He selected aspects of Western culture not contrary to Islam and utilized the principle of public welfare to issue legal decrees (*fatwas*) reforming polygamy, bank interest, and the status of women.

Muhammad Rashid Rida and the *Salafiyya* Movement

Rida carried on Afghani's and 'Abduh's work of reinterpreting Islam and of developing modern institutions and a modern Islamic legal system. However, he was more critical of the growing political and cultural dominance of the West and more influenced by puritanical Wahhabism. He stressed the importance of returning to the model of the pious ancestors (the *salaf*—Muhammad, his Companions, and the first four Caliphs). These had practiced a pure and rational Islam free from superstition and founded a just and prosperous Islamic state. Rida stressed that Islam was a self-sufficient and comprehensive system, which did not need to imitate the West. He also claimed that the full implementation of Islamic law was only possible under a truly Islamic government.

Following Rida, the *Salafiyya* movement was influenced both by the reformist stress on reinterpreting the original sources in order to face the modern world and by Wahhabi Puritanism. It advocated educational and social reforms in order to halt the internal decline of Muslim societies and to gain independence from the West. *Salafis* established schools and welfare programs, published books and magazines, and mobilized the masses in support of the nationalist liberation movements of the time.

Hasan al-Banna and The Muslim Brotherhood

Out of the *Salafiyya* movement emerged the Muslim Brotherhood (1928), the first contemporary fundamentalist mass movement. Founded in Egypt by Hasan al-Banna (1906–1949), it wanted to reform Islam and to improve the condition of the deprived masses by mutual-aid and self-help. Banna saw Islam as an integrated, self-sufficient, and comprehensive social and political system which must be implemented in an Islamic state. There could be no separation between state and religion. It was the implementation of Sharia that made a government truly Islamic, so this implementation was a primary goal of the movement.

The Muslim Brotherhood concentrated first on moral and social reform by establishing educational and welfare programs. Following a period of rapid growth, it became politically active and developed into a tightly knit organization with a network of branches, each subdivided into secret cell groups, and a missionary web that spread into Syria, Palestine, and Sudan. Members received intensive ideological and physical training. Banna outlined a gradualist strategy for achieving power: the preparatory propaganda stage aimed at education; the recruiting and training organizational stage for preparing the ground; and finally the stage of action when the movement implemented its agenda in the state. The strategic objective of the Brotherhood remained constant over the years: to implement Sharia in an Islamic state.

Abul A'la Mawdudi and *Jama'at-i Islami*

On the Indian subcontinent, Abul A'la Mawdudi (1903–1979) was the catalyst for a similar revival. He founded the *Jama'at-i Islami* in 1941 as an elitist organization aimed at establishing an Islamic order. His goal was the complete transformation of individuals, society, and politics in line with Islamic ideology. This transformation would be attained gradually through the efforts of a highly motivated vanguard of enlightened Muslims acting as catalysts of the revolution.

For Mawdudi, Islam was an ideology aimed at dominating the political structures of state and society. Since political power is the only real guarantee for establishing and maintaining pure Islam, he considered it essential for Muslims to be involved in politics and aim at gaining control of the state. The Islamic state is based on the principle that God is the only sovereign ruler and lawgiver. Man, as God's vice-regent on earth, cannot legislate—only interpret and apply God's revealed law. Any submission to man-made rules is idolatry (*shirk*) that sets up man in God's place. Anything that does not conform to Sharia is willful, idolatrous ignorance (*jahiliyya*). Only in cases where Scripture does not give clear guidance is individual interpretation (*ijtihad*) permitted to enact rules that conform to the original intention of God and to the spirit of Islam.

Although Mawdudi attacked the West as degenerate for setting up man as sovereign, thus usurping God's place, he nevertheless disavowed violence and advocated a gradualist approach to achieving power.

Sayyid Qutb

In Egypt, President Nasser (1952–1979), after a brief honeymoon with the Brotherhood, imprisoned and tortured many of its leaders. Sayyid Qutb (1906–1966), the main ideologue of the Muslim Brotherhood, was not only imprisoned and tortured, but later executed by Nasser. However, his writings (especially *Ma'alim fi al-tariq,* translated as "Signposts on the Road" or "Milestones") survived and became the main ideological source of radical Islamic movements, providing them with the criteria by which to judge modern regimes and societies.

Qutb stressed God's unity, sovereignty, and governance as the foundation of the integrated Islamic system. God's inherent unity demands a similar unity in religion, society, and state. As all contemporary societies—including Muslim ones—have reverted to heathen neo-pagan conditions, they are under God's judgment as apostate and their governments must be removed and replaced by true Islamic regimes that will enforce God's law. Accordingly, true believers must withdraw from these corrupt systems and prepare a revolutionary leadership able to take over power in society and state, using force if necessary.

Qutb's revolutionary contribution was his judgment of present-day Muslim societies and regimes as neo-pagan, apostate, and thus legitimate targets for a Holy War (*jihad*). This legitimized violence against any individual, group, or institution labeled apostate. Radical groups were quick to seize on Qutb's theories as the justification for launching terror campaigns against their enemies.

THE THIRD STAGE—AWAKENING (*SAHWA*) AND RADICALISM (1970S AND ONWARDS)

The third stage in Islamic fundamentalism emerged during the 1970s. The disillusionment with tyrannical military regimes, the 1967 defeat in the war against Israel, and the failure of secular ideologies like socialism made Islam appear as the only credible ideology left. Fundamentalist ideas based in familiar Islamic idiom now carried a strong appeal to the disillusioned masses. This new era has been characterized by three main developments: the Islamization of society, the takeover of power by fundamentalists in some states, and the spread of violent groups bent on the destabilization of regimes in Muslim states.

The Spread of Fundamentalist Ideas throughout Society

The spread of fundamentalist ideas across the Muslim world is evident today through increased participation in religious rituals, intensive Mosque building programs, the adoption of Islamic dress by women, the growing of beards by men, and the increased segregation of the sexes. Fundamentalist ideas have come to dominate the media and fundamentalists have gained control of many professional associations and student unions. Charismatic fundamentalist preachers utilizing modern media have become immensely popular, and fundamentalist charitable associations have been founded to serve educational, cultural, healthcare, and poverty-amelioration needs. All of this has created an alternative Islamic society of Islamic neighborhoods, schools, clinics, banks, and mutual-aid networks.

Islamic fundamentalists have become active participators in mainstream Muslim society all over the world. Led by a modern-educated elite, well-versed in Western science and technology, their goal is the implementation of an Islamic system in society and the creation of an Islamic super-state. Islamic fundamentalist movements now operate as a social and political force within the system, and where allowed to operate as political parties, they participate in the democratic process.

Fundamentalists have managed to gain control of some states through violent revolution or *coup d'etat*. Two examples of this trend are Iran and Sudan:

Ruhollah Khomeini and the Iranian Revolution
Shia fundamentalism has been especially centered in Iran and tends to be more clerical and leftist than the Sunni version. Many strands contributed to the movement: clerical opposition to the secularization policies of the Shah; Islamist-Marxist groups like the *fedayan-i Islam* and the *mujahideen–i-khalq* calling for both social justice and Islamic reform; 'Ali Shariati (1933–1977), who greatly impacted Iranian youth with his reinterpretation of Muslim concepts in modern terms, laying the intellectual groundwork for the revolution; and finally Ayatollah Khomeini (1902–1989) who succeeded in pulling these different strands together in order to dramatically change Shia Islam from its traditionally passive mode to an activist revolutionary form.

Ayatollah Khomeini played the role of the brave cleric who fearlessly opposed the illegitimate and unjust ruler. In Shia Islam this arouses messianic fervor linked to the hope of the return of the Hidden Imam, the end-time savior-figure of the faith. Millions were thus radicalized and mobilized to join the mass protests that brought down the Shah's regime in 1979.

Some see the success of the Iranian revolution as the main catalyst for worldwide Islamic fundamentalism, both Sunni and Shia, as it was the first modern state in which Islamic fundamentalism successfully seized power and implemented its vision of true Islam. The establishment of the Islamic Republic in Iran certainly had a great impact on all Shia centers around the Muslim world—Southern Lebanon, Southern Iraq, the Gulf, and the Indian Subcontinent—with Iran becoming the main backer of Shia fundamentalist groups in these areas.

Khomeini's new political concept of Islamic government, the governance by the jurist (*wilayat al-faqih*), claimed that the Hidden Imam is the only legitimate ruler ordained by God and that the highest Shia cleric is his only legitimate representative who ought to rule in his name until his return. A new Islamic constitution was devised adapting Western parliamentary forms to these principles. A parliament was established, but ultimate authority was given to the Supreme Guide, Khomeini.

Hasan al-Turabi and Sudan

Dr. Hasan 'Abdallah al-Turabi began leading the Muslim Brotherhood in Sudan in 1964. After Numayri's downfall in 1985, Turabi's newly founded National Islamic Front (NIF), successor to the Muslim Brotherhood, entered the democratic process and became the third largest party in the 1986 elections. It then participated in the coalition government led by al-Sadiq al-Mahdi. Not content at being a junior partner, it shifted its ideology to instigate and support the military coup of June 1989 which overthrew the democratically elected government and replaced it with the military regime of 'Umar Hasan al-Bashir. While Turabi stressed consultation (*shura*) as an Islamic form of democracy that guarantees pluralism, the NIF actually controlled the reins of power behind al-Bashir and saw to it that all its opponents were dismissed from state and public service. Turabi declared that establishing the Islamic state system in Sudan was the first step towards the ultimate goal of a worldwide Muslim nation (*umma*) under one central Islamic government (*khilafa*).

The Spread of Violent Groups and the Destabilization of Regimes

Since the 1970s, extremist groups have been actively advocating violence and acts of terrorism to destabilize infidel regimes, seize power, and establish an Islamic state by force of arms. Several key examples of this include:

Egypt

Following Nasser's death in 1969, President Sadat manipulated Islamic symbols and encouraged the Muslim Brotherhood to help crush the leftist Nasserist opposition. Islamic associations grew rapidly and penetrated student unions and professional associations. On the fringes of the Brotherhood emerged Qutb's disciples leading violent organizations like the *Jama'at al-Jihad* that assassinated Sadat in 1981. Since then the regime has tried both to co-opt and to suppress the radical groups, but sporadic violence is endemic as radicals attack government security forces, well-known secularists, Coptic Christians, and foreign tourists. Many of their members also joined the *jihads* in Afghanistan, Bosnia, and Chechnya and engaged in international terrorism such as the bombing of the

World Trade Center in New York and the September 11, 2001, atrocities.

Saudi Arabia

Wahhabi Saudi Arabia, which sees itself as the first truly Islamic state in modern times, has been very active in supporting a wide variety of fundamentalist Islamic groups all over the world. It has used its oil wealth to support both moderate and extremist fundamentalist groups in Egypt, Sudan, North Africa, Afghanistan, Central Asia, the Far East, and the West. At the same time, internal dissent has resulted in the rise of fundamentalist opposition groups that accuse the royal family of corruption and hypocrisy and aim at establishing an Islamic Republic in Saudi Arabia. This internal opposition pushes the regime to outflank its criticizers by appearing to be more fundamentalist itself, a vicious cycle that encourages extremism and violence. It is no wonder that Usama bin-Laden and a large proportion of the perpetrators of the September 11, 2001, atrocities were Saudi citizens.

Algeria

In Algeria, the failure of the socialist FLN regime to solve the economic crisis and meet the unfulfilled expectations of the population resulted in the rise of fundamentalist opposition movements calling for social justice in an Islamic framework. They developed links to the Muslim Brotherhood and the radicals in Egypt, to Iran's Islamic Revolution, and to Turabi's regime in Sudan. In the early 1990s the Islamic Salvation Front (FIS) won municipal and parliamentary elections and was on the verge of taking over power democratically when the military intervened. The cancellation of the elections and the prohibition of Islamic parties in 1992 led to a violent civil war, which has taken the lives of almost 100,000 people. While the FIS was originally gradualist, many fringe groups (like the Armed Islamic Group—GIA) drew their inspiration from the Egyptian radicals and advocated indiscriminate violence to break the infidel system and set up an Islamic state.

Afghanistan

The war against the Soviets in Afghanistan was a catalyst for the internationalization of Islamic terror. It began as radical Islamic movements from many countries sent volunteers (Holy Warriors—*mujahideen*) to fight the Soviet occupying forces. Their defeat of the Soviet Union boosted their morale tremendously, while the training and weapons provided by the Pakistani security services, the CIA, and Saudi Arabia turned them into professionals of guerilla warfare and terrorism. Upon their return from Afghanistan, these veterans encouraged a radicalization of Islamic groups and a marked increase in their violent activities. Afghan veterans also fought on other fronts such as Bosnia, Chechnya, and Kossovo, defending threatened Muslim communities against the "Crusading Christian" West.

Following Iraq's invasion of Kuwait, the Gulf War of 1991 further radicalized these groups as they became enraged by the presence of huge "infidel" Western armies in the Arabian Peninsula, the "Holy Land" of Islam.

In the 1990s many extreme movements relocated their centers to the West where they set up bases utilizing the freedom of operation granted them in democratic states. From there they managed far-flung networks and propagated their doctrines back into their home countries by means of modern communication technology and the Internet. Usama bin-Laden's *al-Qa'ida* network was one such movement dedicated to fighting "foreign infidels" from within their own borders.

RESPONSE OF GOVERNMENTS TO FUNDAMENTALISM

Most Muslim states operate under crisis conditions due to the failures of their regimes' secular, nationalist, and socialist programs. The legitimacy of these regimes and elites has been weakened, and opposition is expressed mainly in Islamic idiom.

Government responses to Islamization have been varied and include repression, co-optation, liberalization, and out-Islamizing the Islamists. The violent suppression of fundamentalism has contributed to vicious cycles of violence and counter-violence in countries like Egypt and Algeria. Regimes under pressure have co-opted moderate fundamentalists while suppressing the more radical groups. Some governments tentatively opened up their political systems allowing Islamic parties to participate in elections (Jordan, Morocco, Algeria, Turkey, Egypt, and Tunisia) as well as to join ruling coalitions (Jordan, Pakistan, Malaysia, and Turkey). However, the electoral success of Islamic movements caused governments and military establishments in Algeria, Tunisia, Egypt, and Turkey to change tactics, restricting Islamist political representation or banning it altogether. They accused Islamists of exploiting the democratic system to gain power in order to dismantle democracy and establish totalitarian systems. Iran and Sudan served as negative examples of fundamentalism's rejectionist attitudes toward democracy, pluralism, and the rights of minorities and of women.

The fundamentalist Refah party in Turkey became the largest party in parliament after the elections of 1996 when its leader, Necmetin Erbakan, became Turkey's first Islamist Prime Minister. The military, however, in its role of safeguarding Attaturk's secular legacy, forced Erbakan to resign in 1997 and got the constitutional court to outlaw the Refah party. The long-term results of this move are difficult to predict but might include a radicalization of Islamic groups and a slide back into the violence experienced by Turkey in the 1970s or to that prevalent in Algeria today.

In Pakistan there was a growing trend of Islamization pushed by fundamentalist agitation for an Islamic state based on Sharia. Following the loss of East Pakistan (Bangladesh) and the growing disillusionment with Western-inspired development in the 1960s and 1970s, Bhutto, in spite of his socialist leanings, began to manipulate Islamic symbols and turned to the oil-rich Gulf States for aid. This prepared the ground for Zia's military regime to introduce elements of an Islamic system along Mawdudi's lines. Pakistan's deep involvement in Afghanistan, backing the Sunni mujahideen and later the Taliban, and its backing of similar fundamentalist guerillas in Kashmir, served to strengthen its own Islamic fundamentalist groups. Increased violence between competing groups, against Pakistani Christians and Westerners, and between Sunni and Shia extremists marked this development.

Shia Fundamentalism

While sharing some common roots with Sunni revivalism, Shia fundamentalism went its own specific way, drawing inspiration from Iran and tending to be more clerical and leftist than its Sunni counterpart. Several factors contributed to this shift away from its traditionally passive mode toward an activist and revolutionary stance, including: clerical opposition to the secularizing policies of Reza Shah and Muhammad Reza Shah in Iran, the activities of Islamist-Marxists, the Sufi-existentialist ideology of 'Ali Shariati (1933–1977), and the rise of Ayatollah Khomeini (1902–1989). 'Ali Shariati laid the intellectual groundwork for the revolution while Ayatollah Khomeini took on the traditional eschatological role of the brave cleric (representing the Hidden Imam) opposing the corrupt tyrant. Khomeini initiated a shift from the passive cult of venerating the Hidden Imam while awaiting his return, to an active program in which the ruling clerics and jurists implemented their interpretations of Islamic law and their views of radical Islam as the Imam's legitimate representatives. Khomeini succeeded in mobilizing the masses with a messianic fervor against the Shah's regime, resulting in millions joining the mass protests that finally brought it down in 1979.

The Shia regime following the revolution was very different from the Sunni version of an Islamic state but suited to millenarian Shia expectations of the return and rule of the Hidden Imam. Khomeini's innovative ideology of the Islamic state (*wilayat al-faqih*) demanded that the highest Islamic jurist, as the legitimate representative of the Hidden Imam, rule in his name until his return. The establishment of the Islamic Republic in Iran had a great impact on all Shia centers around the Muslim world.

The success of the Iranian revolution was an important catalyst for worldwide Islamic fundamentalism, both Sunni and Shia, as it was the first modern state in which Islamic fundamentalism succeeded in taking over power and implementing its vision of puritan Islam. The new Islamic state formulated an Islamic constitution with appropriate institutions and changed the economic system to be more in line with Islamist principles, thus offering a model to fundamentalists struggling to attain power in other states.

Following Khomeini's death the regime entered a consolidation phase, balancing its revolutionary fervor with the necessities of developing functional governmental institutions, balancing the various pressure groups within the new ruling elite, and creating better international relations. The election of Khatami as president in 1997 points to a shift to moderation and pragmatism among the population, though the hardliners in power successfully blocked attempts at real liberalization. Iran is now trying to consolidate its power, assert its influence in the Middle East, the Caucasus, and Central Asia, while reaching some accommodation with rivals such as Saudi Arabia and the United States. However, Iran is still the main backer of Shia fundamentalist groups in the Islamic world, especially in Lebanon and Afghanistan.

CONCLUSION

Though Islamic reform began as a spiritual and intellectual battle to remove the causes of weakness and decadence in Muslim societies, it gave birth to a radical fundamentalist version that searched for scapegoats on whom to lay the blame for the calamities afflicting Muslims. The first scapegoats to be identified were the corrupt regimes and institutions in Muslim states and societies, but the list was later expanded to include Western power—*especially* the United States.

Islamic fundamentalism emerged as part of the Islamic reform movement. Fundamentalists rejected the blind imitation of traditionalist scholars and the superstitious accretions of medieval Islam. While some modernists and liberals sought to reform Islam by emulating Western models in philosophy, science, and politics, the fundamentalists were intent on emulating the Prophet and his Companions. They demanded a return to the source texts, the privilege of reinterpretation (*ijtihad*), and the reintegration of politics within a total Islamic system (Sharia). To achieve their goal of transforming Muslim society, they aimed at acquiring political power so as to set up true Islamic states.

Reformist energies are currently being directed toward venting all the frustrations of the past few centuries of dependency and humiliation on those identified as scapegoats. This appeals to populist notions of shame, wounded pride, and the loss of honor being redeemable only by the shedding of blood, and it plays into revolutionary Third World concepts and Islamic messianic traditions.

Tragically, the indiscriminate shedding of blood has become the hallmark of Islamic fundamentalist movements that have diverged from the mainstream in determining to achieve their aims by force through revolution, *coup d'etats*, or terrorism. By using heretical Muslim paradigms to reinterpret traditional concepts, these groups have justified indiscriminate violence against all perceived enemies, Muslim and non-Muslim, as contemporary headlines confirm on an almost daily basis.

3

"Scripture Only!"

GETTING BACK TO THE SOURCE

INTRODUCTION

"Scripture Only" (*sola scriptura*) was a rallying cry of the Reformation, calling Christians to abandon all other added sources of authority and revert to the original apostolic teaching of revealed Scripture, the Bible, as the inspired word of God that alone had final authority in all matters of doctrine and practice. Islamic fundamentalists, following the reform movements of the last two centuries, have formulated a similar demand to return to the Quran (the written revelation given to Muhammad) and Sunna (the authoritative collection of Muhammad's words and deeds) as the only and final source of authority within Islam. They thus reject the authority (though not necessarily the usefulness) of later interpretations, commentaries, and legal enactments.

All fundamentalists see their Scriptures as the axiomatically true revelation of God's will for humanity to which all humans must submit and obey. As Scripture is God's inspired revelation, it is inerrant and carries absolute authority as the framework for all human activities.

There are some resemblances in the way evangelicals and Islamic fundamentalists describe their Scriptures. Both see them as infallible, unchanging, reliable, divinely preserved, and applicable for all times and places. Both stress the necessity of God revealing himself in Scripture to meet the human need for true knowledge of God and for guidance in all areas of life. Both demand that believers must return to the original sources and apply them to modern contexts. Both decry later deviations and additional sources of authority as wrong and corrupting.

There are, of course, differences as well. Evangelicals attribute divine inerrancy only to the original manuscripts (with present-day copies and translations being reasonably reliable versions of the original), while Islamic fundamentalists attribute absolute inerrancy and perfection to the copies of the Quran in their hands today. They stress the traditional Muslim view of the Quran handed down by God to humanity as a perfect counterpart of the heavenly version. While evangelicals regard only the Bible as inspired Scripture, most Muslims also accept Hadith (the various collections of narratives about Muhammad that constitute Sunna) as part of their claimed inspired Scripture. The Islamic view of the Quran is similar to the Christian view of Christ as the eternal, uncreated living word of God, while the Islamic view of Hadith is similar to the evangelical view of the Bible, both acknowledging a mingling of the human and the divine in compilation, affirming a divine overruling of the process, and an ongoing divine preservation of the canon.

THE CENTRALITY AND ULTIMATE AUTHORITY OF SCRIPTURE

Islamic fundamentalists claim that because their Scriptures are divinely revealed they are the ultimate authority for doctrine and practice and the absolute moral standard. For most Muslims, not only fundamentalists, the Quran is unquestionably God's word with no need to discuss the subject. However, Islamic fundamentalists deny the final authority of later commentators and interpreters that are accepted by traditionalists.

God's revelation in the Quran is seen as necessary as it offers humans the perfect way to salvation and success. Muslim Scripture is the only revelation given to humanity by which to establish God's rule on earth.[38] "God's book" is the ultimate authority and believers must renounce all other authorities and judge all things by the Quran and Sunna only.

> The moment you recite the *kalimah*[39] you accept that the only law you recognize is God's law, only God is your sovereign, only God is your ruler, you will obey only God, only the things written in God's book and given by his Messenger. You renounce all other authority in favor of God's authority, you judge everything in the light of Qur'an and Sunnah: accept what conforms to them, reject what contradicts them.[40]

The Quran is accepted as the necessary guide for humans in an evil world,[41] the sole provision for the spiritual life of humanity and for the establishment of a perfect social and religious world order.[42]

INSPIRATION, INERRANCY, PRESERVATION

Islamic fundamentalists stress the uncreatedness, divine origin, and nature of the Quran as God's word.[43] As the Quran is God's own word, it follows that God will see to its perfect preservation since first given to Muhammad.[44] They defend the divine inspiration of their Scriptures, their uniqueness and authority, claiming these are completely trustworthy, uncorrupted, free from error, always relevant, and applicable to all times and places. The Quran was given so humans could become pious, God-conscious, and able to differentiate between right and wrong. It is as relevant today as it was when first given: "As you read the Qur'an, Allah speaks to you. To read the Qur'an is to hear Him, even to converse with Him, and to walk in His ways. It is the encounter of life with the Life-giver."[45]

Islamic fundamentalists claim that the Quran and Sunna in their original purity are the only true source of Islam, as all other traditions are infected by human error. Scripture is the only reliable guide for humanity in all its affairs for all of time, dealing with the most basic questions facing humans—their relationship to God. When needing divine guidance, believers must turn to the pure sources of the Quran and Hadith.[46] Everything else is "buried under the debris of man-made traditions . . . crushed under those false laws and customs that are not even remotely related to the Islamic teachings."[47]

Fundamentalists claim that the Quran and Sunna together are the only reliable sources in the world for knowing God's will, as in them God, by direct revelation, imparted all the instructions he wished to communicate to humanity. The Quran exists today exactly as originally revealed—not a word or a syllable have been altered. It is the word of God in the original text preserved for all time, addressed to all mankind in all ages as the eternal standard for human life.[48] The Hadith provide an accurate record of the life and sayings of the Muhammad: "There has not been an iota of change in this unique historic record. ... The sayings and the entire record of the life of the Holy Prophet have been handed down to us with unprecedented precision and authenticity in works of the Hadith and the *Sira*."[49]

THE RIGHT ATTITUDE TO SCRIPTURE

Like evangelicals, Islamic fundamentalists teach the importance of the right attitudes of faith, submission, and humility in a person's approach to Scripture, coupled to a willingness to implement its teachings as soon as they are understood. God has spoken clearly and finally in Scripture and the real question is whether humans are willing to submit to God and obey his word rather than follow their own desires.[50] Humans are urged to let Scripture speak to them directly, transforming them from within as they integrate its message into their lives, Scripture being the motivator to action and to revolutionary change. The right attitude to the Quran is one of self-surrender and obedience as only what is practiced is of any value. A true Muslim builds his life around the Quran, devoting himself totally to its study and to obeying its message. The right approach to the Quran is one of gratitude to God for giving it, faith in it as the word of God, purity of intention in accepting its teachings and guidance, and a willingness to obey its injunctions and to be changed by its teachings.[51]

Studying the Quran is not a matter of learning theology but of putting scriptural beliefs into practice, implementing them in a comprehensive system for a living community.[52] The Quran will only reveal its treasures to the one who studies it with the intention of acting upon it. True Muslims ought to emulate the unique

Companions of the Prophet in Islam's "golden age" who studied Scripture determined to immediately obey its rules and were changed into living examples of a faith powerful enough to change the world.[53]

Some writers warn against hypocrisy in attitudes to the Quran. True faith is expressed not by verbally proclaiming it to be the word of God but by heartfelt devotion to its teachings. Muslims must study it carefully, reflect on its message, seek its guidance, and act upon its teachings in every sphere.[54]

THE INTERPRETATION OF SCRIPTURE

Traditional Islam apportioned the right of official interpretation of Scripture to clerical experts (*ulama*) who followed traditional commentaries and precedents to arrive at their legal rulings. Islamic fundamentalists, on the other hand, give every Muslim the right to interpret and apply Scripture without needing professional intermediaries.[55] The right method is that of letting the Quran interpret itself, placing the literal meaning in its historical context and applying it to real life situations. All rules of faith and conduct must be derived directly from the Muslim Scriptures. Where directly related texts are not available, independent, individual interpretation (*ijtihad*) is permitted—this contrasts with the traditional view of the gates of *ijtihad* being closed in the early centuries of Islam. Reason is useful in interpretation, but it must be subordinated to revelation. Some stress that while it is the potential right of every believer to interpret Scripture for himself, only those who "use their God-given faculty of reason to acquire the appropriate knowledge" are actually qualified to do so, thus limiting the egalitarian principle.[56]

The fundamentals of Islam are found in a few straightforward

Quranic passages, and from these basic principles all the many practical rules for daily life are easily developed. It is wrong to quote Quranic texts out of context or to use them as isolated proof texts. The text determines how human reason ought to interpret it, not the other way round.[57] The basic guidance is permanent, but its application changes according to the peculiar needs of every generation. Revelation is given to help humans determine between right and wrong and all are obliged to implement its requirements in every sphere. Conducting all human affairs according to Scripture is the ultimate test of acceptance by God.[58]

Some fundamentalists stress that God's revelation in the Quran and Sunna deals mainly with essential laws that must be interpreted and applied to concrete situations in real life, and that all believers ought to be active in the process of extracting the divine ruling for each specific case.[59] There is no need for ordained official clergy in this process of interpretation as every Muslim is personally responsible to God and has the right of interpretation. There is a difference between the scriptural text and its interpretation, as interpretation is a fallible human process and its results are not 'the Revelation' but rather the interpreter's understanding of revelation on the specific point in question.[60]

As to later commentators and interpreters, there is a variety of attitudes. One extreme position is that taken by the radical Egyptian group *Jama'at al-Takfir wal-Hijra* which repudiated all interpretations after the first four righteous Caliphs, including the four Islamic schools of law (*madhabs*) and traditional commentators. These were all unnecessary, as the Quran was given in plain Arabic that every one can understand, and there was no need for mediators between God and believers.[61]

In contrast, the Egyptian *Jama'at al-Jihad*[62] (responsible for the assassination of President Sadat), while calling for a return to the Quran and Sunna, accepted the four *madhabs*, much interpretation which had scholarly consensus, and some later commentators.[63]

Shia fundamentalists have a less literalist interpretation of Scripture than Sunnis, stressing the many layers of meaning in the Quran. Interpretation is viewed more as the domain of the Shia clerical class. Khomeini, for example, argued that the Quran has many layers of meaning, some of which may never be understood. No one is allowed to claim "the Quran says so," only that this is his interpretation of the Quran on this point: "When I explain any verse of the Quran, I do not claim that the verse means only what I say. I do not say anything for certain. I am hinting at a possibility only."[64] Shias also claim that the Quran is written in symbolic language and has hidden meanings in addition to the direct and literal meaning, its multiple levels containing all truth for all time.[65]

SCRIPTURE AS LAW

Most evangelicals would agree that God's will is revealed in Scripture and that it is the duty of believers to obey God's will as revealed, seeking to please him in all their thoughts and deeds. Evangelicals tend to argue among themselves as to the extent of scriptural law, some stressing grace and freedom as against law, viewing Scripture mainly as a source of broad moral guidelines, others accepting the whole Bible as God's law valid in many of its detailed instructions for the contemporary world.

Islamic fundamentalists, on the other hand, strongly stress that the claimed revealed divine law, Sharia, based on the Muslim Scriptures, is a total and complete system binding on individuals, society, and the state in all its details. Sharia serves as an important identity marker for Muslims. While other religions believe in God and his prophets, only Muslims possess Sharia as a comprehensive body of law and a powerful symbol of a truly integrated society in stark contrast to the fragmented modern Western societies.[66]

Islamic fundamentalists state that the Quran teaches the basics of Islam, while the Quran and Sunna together contain the legal code, Sharia, which must be followed by Muslims in all its moral and ritual details. Fundamentalists differ on various aspects of these rules, discussing which customs are regional traditions and which are literal injunctions of Sharia. This variety of opinion is clearly exemplified in the differences between the application of Sharia by the Taliban of Afghanistan, Islamic Iran, and Saudi-Arabia. Each lays a different emphasis on the status and role of women in society, differing on women's educational and employment possibilities, involvement in politics and public life, as well as on the proscribed dress patterns and the extent to which segregation of the sexes must be maintained.

Islamic fundamentalists see Sharia as a "protective fence" within which believers can lead a safe life. The essentials of Islamic law specified in the Quran and practiced by the Prophet and his Companions are obligatory on all. There are various lists of the essential rules, among them the five pillars, *jihad*, the commanding of good and the forbidding of evil, the obtaining of education, good deportment and high moral values, care of physical health, and social solidarity. There are also many rules concerning ritual purity and pollution. Fundamentalists demand that legislation in Muslim states be derived from the prescriptions of Sharia,[67] and many demand that Islamic law be the sole legal system of the Islamic state, serving both as constitution and legal code.

Sharia is seen as God's comprehensive total system of law, a summary of all God has prescribed for humanity in all spheres, including fundamental doctrines, norms of behavior, principles of government, economic guidelines, and essentials of knowledge.[68] Usurping God's legislative authority is the greatest sin of the modern world because only God, the absolute ruler of the universe, has the right to legislate for humanity. Humans may only interpret and apply God's law. As humans are subject to God's laws in nature, so they must voluntarily submit themselves to God's laws in Scripture. God's law establishes harmony and equilibrium not just in human society but also in the whole cosmos. For radicals, any group, society, or regime that fails to implement Sharia must be declared apostate and ought to be destroyed and replaced by a true Islamic society following the model of Muhammad's government in Medina.[69]

4

"Come Out from Their Midst and Be Separate"[70]

SEPARATION, MIGRATION, AND CONQUEST

INTRODUCTION

All fundamentalists are puritan separatists in their stress on personal moral separation from evil and on the struggle against it. Most set visible boundaries and demand a visible demarcation from worldly society and its corrupting influences. These boundaries are typically expressed in strict norms of conduct, dress, and behavior. Some demand institutional separation from both the world and erring believers in order to ensure doctrinal and institutional purity. A few go so far as to demand total separation from all aspects of evil society and the corrupt state.

These degrees of separation can easily be seen among Christian fundamentalists. Though the entire movement tends to stress doctrinal and ecclesiastical separation, some groups emphasize the need to separate from society and politics altogether, while others advocate wholehearted involvement in both.

ISLAMIC VIEWS ON SEPARATION—
DEVELOPMENT IN STAGES

While fundamentalist Christians seek to separate from evil in all its manifestations in society, churches, doctrine, and apostate institutions, Islamic fundamentalists concentrate on the degree of separation from *jahili* (pagan, ignorant) society and view separation as a stage in the political quest for the establishment of the Islamic state modeled on Muhammad's practice.

Qutb reinterpreted the concepts of separation (*mufassala*) and migration (*hijra*) by arguing that the first model Muslim community had developed in clearly defined stages that must be emulated today. First was the proclamation of the message, then the separation (*mufassala*) from unbelievers, and finally the fight to implement God's new society on earth. Separation from *jahili* society is a necessary step for establishing boundaries. It is not conceived of as total physical separation, but—like the Christian engagement concept—as a spiritual separation while remaining in society to proclaim and recruit. When a person became a Muslim during the Islamic golden age, he made a clean break with his past, separating himself totally from the *jahili* environment and starting a new life with the Quran as his only guide. This characteristic of the first unique generation is a necessary condition for any modern renewal. The first step for revival is separation from *jahili* society, followed by immersion in the Quran, a process that will transform Muslims and enable them to radically change society.[71]

In the first stages of the process leading to the replacement of all human systems with the God-given revolutionary system of Islam, total separation is, however, not deemed possible. Qutb here adopts a stand somewhat similar to the Christian principle of "in the world, but not of it":

> This cannot come about by going along even a few steps with *jahiliyyah,* nor by severing relations with it and removing ourselves to a separate corner; never. *The correct procedure is to mix with discretion, give and take with dignity; speak the truth with love, and show the superiority of the Faith with humility.* But we must always bear in mind that we live in the midst of *jahiliyyah,* that our way of life is nobler than that of *jahiliyya,* and that the change from *jahiliyyah* to Islam is vast and far-reaching.[72]

Physical Separation

Takfir wal-Hijra, a radical Egyptian movement, developed Qutb's ideas on separation to mean that all true Muslims in all generations must emulate Muhammad's model of *hijra* (migration) from Mecca to Medina: there must be physical separation from unbelieving society, withdrawal to a safe location to establish a new alternative society, and preparations for the stage of *tamakkun* (strength) and ultimate victory. Total separation is an absolute necessity in the temporary stage of weakness that ends when the alternative community becomes strong enough to challenge the regime. *Takfir* was a millenarian movement which aimed at winning over a large portion of the Egyptian population before it would deem itself strong enough for the final assault on *jahili* society. Separation was interpreted as meaning that society members refused to be conscripted into the army and felt no allegiance to the state, rejecting anything that might serve its interests. In case of war, members must not fight in the ranks of the Egyptian Army but flee to secure positions. They did not recognize state education, uniforms, marriage, or legal systems—since all was *jahili*. They were not allowed to be state employees, and those who were, changed jobs on entering the society.[73]

Spiritual Separation

Al-Jihad, another radical group, rejected the notion of total separation from society, interpreting Qutb's concept of separation as purely spiritual and moral, with a duty laid on true believers to penetrate the structures of *jahili* society in order to bring about a radical change as soon as possible. *Al-Jihad* tried to infiltrate the military, security services, and government institutions so as to wage immediate *jihad*.[74]

These early Egyptian radical movements continue to serve as models for contemporary extremist groups who emulate their ideologies and lifestyle and implement them in their strategies and tactics.

5

"For the Lord Is Our Judge, the Lord Is Our Lawgiver, the Lord Is Our King"[75]

THE UNITY AND SOVEREIGNTY OF GOD

INTRODUCTION

Secularism and liberal humanism have placed man at the center of their worldview and at the center of the universe. In contrast, Islamic fundamentalism (like evangelicalism) is God-centered, accepting God's existence, uniqueness, and sovereignty as an axiomatic presupposition and claiming God's revelation in Muslim Scriptures as the only basis of all truth, knowledge, and morality. Islamic fundamentalists believe in a theocentric universe in which God's sovereign rule and divinely revealed will are central. Man's place in this universe is in a covenantal position of submission, dependence, and obedience to God. The real cause of man-centered secularism is the rebellious attitude of the human heart against the self-evident truths of God's uniqueness and revelations through nature and Muhammad. Man is expected to submit to God and obey his revelation, not to question and doubt.

GOD'S UNITY (*TAWHID*)

Islamic fundamentalists, like most Muslims, stress the doctrine of God's unity (*tawhid*) as the foundation of Islam. The one God created everything according to his inscrutable and absolute will. The universe is created as a unified and harmonious whole, preserved and ordered by God.[76] For Islamic fundamentalists, God's unity implies that there is only one God-approved law (Sharia) and one correct political model for human society, as God's absolute indivisible unity must be replicated in human society and politics. Fundamentalists feel duty bound to establish an integrated social and political order on earth that mirrors the divine order in heaven and in nature.

The unity of the created universe permeates the whole cosmos, ensuring an integrated harmony and equilibrium of all creation. Every existing thing has an intrinsic value and is in harmony with the whole universe. As God's vice-regents on earth, human beings have the duty to obey God's laws in nature and in revelation so as to bring harmony to the universe. However, since humans are endowed by God with the gift of free will, they have the potential to disturb this primeval unity. Qutb argued that the cosmic equilibrium has been upset because many Muslims exchanged the true faith for secularism. Repairing this damage and restoring the harmony of the universe requires a reintegration of the two aspects of God's law, Sharia and the laws of nature, reclaiming their essential unity and repairing the torn cosmos, thus restoring man to his proper place.[77]

Fundamentalists see the Creator God as the real source of order in the created universe that is not divided into warring elements but is an integrated whole governed by God's one omnipotent will.[78] The concept of the unity of God is accepted as the most revolutionary doctrine of Islam. When man submits to this concept, he is freed from slavery to evil and to irrational and demonic powers, receives a meaningful worldview, and is given a position of great dignity. By accepting the role of God's slave, man becomes master of creation under God.[79]

Tawhid is thus accepted as the very essence of Islam, a revolutionary concept that presents a unified and integrated worldview. It assures the supremacy of law in the cosmos and points to the all-pervading unity behind the manifest diversity. Fundamentalists teach that it is a dynamic doctrine of the unity and equality of all men without distinction that condemns all barriers and guarantees true freedom.[80] For Ayatollah Sayyid Ali Khamenei, Iran's Supreme Guide, *tawhid* is the basis of Islam's revolutionary worldview. Parallel to the unity of the Creator is the fact that all created things are elements of one set, the universe, a unit with one God-given direction. Khamenei uses the parable of camels in a caravan linked by chains, working together and for each other, and in so doing, finding their true meaning and rightful place in the total picture, realizing that no one in this universe is independent.[81]

On a more mystical note, Shariati sees the whole cosmos as one living self-conscious organism evolving in a pre-determined direction toward a utopian goal. No matter what reality seems like, *tawhid* states that the universe is a harmonious whole and it is man's responsibility to accept this model of reality and move with its flow. The seeming discord of this world is not a result of an inherent flaw in God's creation but of opposing idolatrous worldviews (*shirk*) imposed on the universe by men who reject the *tawhidic* model. Instead of accepting the God-given unity of creation, *shirk* sees the cosmos as full of conflicting forces.

GOD'S SOVEREIGN GOVERNANCE (*HAKIMIYYA*)

Muslim traditionalists would agree with the fundamentalist concepts of God's unity, but the unique fundamentalist contribution is the insistence on a conscious, literal, and active contemporary application of this doctrine not only to personal life but also to contemporary society and state, transforming it from a creedal belief to a revolutionary ideology and practical political program. The individual must consciously accept God as his sole rightful owner, the sole object of his worship, and the sole lawgiver.[82] Everything in the universe, including man, belongs to God and must submit to his authority. Believers acknowledge no other master or sovereign, as God alone is worthy of worship and service.[83]

As God is the only sovereign in the universe, there can be no competing human sovereignty of people or parliament. Man must submit to God's revealed law and is not allowed to legislate, only to interpret and apply God's law. All independent human legislation is a rebellious usurpation of God's prerogative and thus the essence of evil. Man's total submission to God and to God's law frees him from submission to any other power and places all believers as equals before God under his law.

Qutb stressed that the main attribute of God's uniqueness is his sovereignty (*hakimiyya*) to which man is obliged to surrender and submit. Linked to this is the doctrine of the lordship of God (*rabbaniyya*) that distinguishes Islam from all human ideologies.[84] God's sole authority must be established on earth and all rebellion must be eradicated from its face. Islam is based on the truth that all authority belongs to God alone: "There is no sovereignty except Allah's, no law except from Allah, and no authority of one man over another, because all authority belongs to God alone."[85] Only God has ultimate sovereignty and authority over the whole universe including humanity and its affairs. The Islamic state must be based on the principle that all authority belongs to God alone and must establish a political system (*manhaj*) that expresses God's sovereignty by being based on Sharia. It is thus fundamentally different from all human systems of government.

Politically, this fundamentalist concept of God's sovereignty means that individuals and states must totally submit to God's sovereign rule by fully implementing Sharia. All laws, rules, and judgments must be derived from Sharia and from nothing else. Implementation of Sharia thus became the sole criterion of legitimacy—anything less is a reversion to the evil state of ignorance existing in pre-Islamic pagan Arabia (*jahiliyya*).[86]

The sovereignty of God is total with nothing left outside his lordship. Whoever sets himself up as an independent agent defies God and becomes an idol or a tyrant (*taghut*) assuming God's rightful place. In secular states God has been totally rejected, rulers having usurped his place as omnipotent and absolute alternative gods.[87] They have thus reverted to idolatry and this is the real problem facing the modern world.[88]

Somewhat similar to Christian liberation theology, Shariati adds a Marxist dimension by transforming the traditional doctrine of God's unity into the ideological basis of revolution. History is the eternal dialectical struggle between *tawhid* and *shirk*. *Tawhid* is the "natural" God-given order of things, while *shirk* is the enemy who has to be fought and eliminated. *Tawhid* means submission to God alone and a revolt against all other powers: "In tawhid man fears only one power, is answerable to one judge, turns only to one qibla, directs his hopes to only one source."[89]

Islamic fundamentalists have thus transformed *tawhid* into a revolutionary political ideology that radically rejects the right of anyone but God to rule over human society.[90] It is not just a theory but a political, social, and economic tool for a revolutionary remaking of society according to God's will while opposing and destroying all *jahili* powers.[91] True *tawhid* cannot tolerate any competitors to God; it makes the existence of pagan conditions unbearable and motivates the revolutionary desire to overthrow them and to set up a new socio-economic and political order centered on God's sovereign rule.[92] Radicals reject Western political concepts of the sovereignty of the people and the division of powers. This, unfortunately, opens the door to totalitarian systems in which leaders can gain absolute power by claiming to represent God and his will. Moderate fundamentalists have realized this danger and are trying to grapple with these issues in their discussions.

6

"On Earth As It Is in Heaven"[93]

THE GOD-PLEASING STATE

INTRODUCTION

Many evangelical Christians opt for passive non-involvement in politics due to the lack of political prescriptions in the New Testament. Islamic fundamentalists, on the other hand, interpret Muslim Scriptures as endorsing political activism. For Islamic fundamentalists, politics are simply efforts to establish a God-centered and a God-guided community according to their interpretations of Islamic law. God holds the ultimate divine authority and sovereignty, but he delegates some authority to humans who are therefore accountable to him. All human institutions and offices are limited by God in their scope and must be exercised within the specific parameters set out for them in Muslim Scriptures. Political authority is not independent or autonomous but bound by the principles revealed in the divine law (Sharia), in contradiction of which it may neither legislate nor act.

Islamic fundamentalists criticize traditional Islam for being too passive, and they press for an activist engagement in society and politics in order to bring about desired changes. Islam is treated like a revolutionary political ideology, a political tool for transforming society and state. Islamic fundamentalists have actually borrowed much from modern Western totalitarian political ideologies—Fascism, Nazism, and Marxism—translating secular concepts into Islamic language. They use propaganda and conspiracy theories in a similar manner and favor totalitarian systems that control all aspects of life.

As to the divinely prescribed relationship between religion and state, Christians face the divergence between the Old Testament's theocratic covenant model and the New Testament's relative silence on political matters. Some uphold various Old Testament models as still valid today, while others believe the apolitical New Testament stand supersedes that of the Old Testament. In contrast, Islamic fundamentalists are unanimous in claiming that their Scriptures prescribe the unity of state and religion and the setting up of an Islamic state. They lay great emphasis on the state as the main tool for implementing true Islam in the world. Their efforts are therefore concentrated on capturing the state and its centers of power, either legally within the democratic process or violently by revolution or coup. Stressing the paramount importance of believers being involved in politics, they are divided as to the exact form of the Islamic state prescribed. Should it be an exact copy of Muhammad's original model in Medina with huge powers given to the ruler (*khalifa*)? Or, would a flexible reinterpretation of the original with some characteristics of a modern democratic system be better?

POLITICS SUBORDINATE TO RELIGION— IMPLEMENT *SHARIA*

Islamic fundamentalists declare that for human political authority to be legitimate it must be rooted in God as the ultimate sovereign, emanate from him, and enforce his law—Sharia. Any government that does not rule by God's Sharia alone is illegitimate to some extent.[94]

As to the desired legal system in the state, evangelicals differ from each other because they face the dichotomy of freedom from the law by God's grace contrasted with the Old Testament system of laws applying to the state. Evangelical views on this subject range from the Calvinist view of biblical law being applicable to the state, to the more general view of biblical moral law (such as the Ten Commandments) as the basis of the state legal system, to the non-conformist view of total non-involvement in state politics and legal systems.

Islamic fundamentalists argue that the legal system in the Islamic state must be the Sharia and loudly demand its implementation in all Muslim-majority states. However, they disagree among themselves as to whether it is to be applied to Muslims only or to all of society, whether it is to be literally implemented in every detail, or whether the state legal system should be based on a flexible reinterpretation and reapplication of its essential principles. They also discuss the need for ongoing interpretation (*ijtihad*) to adapt it to modern contexts. These discussions form the basis of the differences between the legal systems of fundamental Islamic states like Iran, Saudi Arabia, and Afghanistan under the Taliban, each state claiming it has the best implementation of Islamic law.

Given the symbolic importance of the Sharia legal system for fundamentalists, its political implementation in the state has become the real criterion for the legitimacy of all regimes and societies. Sharia has become the fundamentalist substitute for the central criteria of secular ideologies—like the "dictatorship of the proletariat" was for communists or racial purity for the Nazis. It is the touchstone by which everything else is judged, the sole criterion of legitimacy.

The concept of *"hakimiyya,"* sovereignty belonging to God alone, means that individuals and states must totally submit to God's sovereign rule by fully implementing Sharia. All laws, rules, and judgments must be derived from Sharia and from nothing else. They must be established either from a clear authoritative text where one exists or by means of *ijtihad* (the right of every pious Muslim to personally interpret the Muslim Scriptures) within the bounds of generally accepted interpretative principles when no authoritative text is available. Anything less is rebellion against God's sovereign rule and is classed as *jahiliyya* (heathen lawlessness) demanding harsh reprisals. In the true Islamic system:

> The divinity of God (S) must be realized on earth as this divinity is realized in heaven; it must be realized through submission to His Shari'ah and command just as it is realized through his foreordaining and determining of events.[95]

This ideology is the source of the insistent demand for the full implementation of Sharia in many states with large Muslim communities from Nigeria to Sudan to Indonesia. This is also the basis for the pronouncement by radicals of present regimes as pagan (*takfir*) and therefore legitimate targets of violence.

POLITICAL GOALS

The political goal of Islamic fundamentalists is the Islamization of the total social and political systems of their societies and states, along with the establishment of a universal true Islamic state following the prophetic model in which Sharia is law. Hasan al-Banna, founder of the Muslim Brotherhood, defined the ultimate goal of Islamic politics as "the resurrection of the Islamic empire as a unified state embracing the scattered peoples of the Islamic world, raising the banner of Islam and bearing its message."

Banna saw Muslims as guardians of humanity commissioned to instruct all mankind in God's ways. The best way to do this is by providing a universal Islamic political and legal framework of Sharia in which all can experience its benefits, justice, and effectiveness. According to this utopian view, the implementation of Sharia will produce permanent peace, the raising of the standard of living, the imposition of good Islamic practices, and the wiping out "with full force all those evils of which Islam aims to cleanse mankind of."[96]

Mawdudi, the founder of *Jama'at-i Islami* in Pakistan, states that an important goal of the Islamic state is to present a visible witness to the world of a society functioning on the basis of God's principles and translating them into public policies and programs. This utopian society has a caring and efficient administration that ensures law and order as well as equitable social welfare because of the high morality of its public servants. It practices virtue in internal policies and honesty in foreign policies. It conducts war in a civilized manner and exhibits integrity and loyalty in peace. It is thus a model and a living testimony for all humanity to see that Islam is the true guarantor of human well-being.[97]

Another political goal is the removal of God's enemies from political rule thus liberating mankind from tyranny. Qutb claimed that Islam's primary goal, as the only worldwide system ordained by God, is "to remove *jahiliyya* from the position of authority and to take the lead into its own hands in order to promulgate its own special way of life . . . to replace this *jahiliyya* with Islamic ideas and traditions."[98] This calls for the establishment of an Islamic state operating an Islamic system (*nizam Islami*) and governed by Islamic law, Sharia.[99]

Islam is a God-given revolutionary system aimed at totally replacing all other human systems. This is to be achieved through a step-by-step program of first inviting everyone to Islam, then propagating true Islam among the masses, and finally establishing the Islamic state.[100]

Among the more radical Islamic movements, the goal is clearly stated as being the re-establishment of the original worldwide Caliphate along the lines of the first four "righteous" Caliphs who followed Muhammad. The Conference of Islamic Revivalist Movements, organized by the *Al-Muhajiroun* movement in London in November 1998, stated in its final declaration: "The Islamic Movements agree that the global problems we face are the direct result of the absence of the Islamic State (Al-Khilafah) and the need to co-operate and work together to fulfill the duty of its re-establishment."[101] Egypt's *al-Jama'a al-Islamiyya* states that while its first goal is to bring all mankind into submission to God, the second goal is the establishment of a *khilafa* on the model of the Prophet.[102]

Islamic fundamentalists thus clearly demand the active political participation of all true Muslims in a worldwide program aimed at the imposition of Islamic political and legal systems in all countries and the unification of all Muslim countries into one Islamic super state under a ruler with the title of Caliph. They express the utopian conviction that the very act of establishing an Islamic Sharia state will automatically solve all problems of evil because it has the guarantee of God's blessing and because the state officers will be pious Muslims who have the best of the community at heart and who can do no wrong. This utopian nature of Islamic fundamentalism is based on a utopian view of the nature of man that ignores the reality of sin and evil. Rather, they believe that providing perfect external conditions will ensure the virtue of all individuals, thereby eliminating the need for checks and balances in the political system. (The existence of checks and balances in Western democratic systems is largely due to the biblical views of original sin and the depravity of human nature. Such views demand carefully planned mechanisms to keep evil in check, such as term limits to guard against corruption by power and procedures for removing corrupt officials from office.)

7

"Professing to Be Wise, They Became Fools"[103]

DEALING WITH CONTEMPORARY NEO-PAGANISM

INTRODUCTION

When Paul was in Athens he was disturbed by the symbols of idolatry that filled the city. In his speech to the Athenians on the Areopagus, he proclaimed that a new era had arrived in which God was initiating a dispensation for humanity in Christ. Referring to the old pagan days that were passing away, he said: "Therefore having overlooked the **times of ignorance**, God is now declaring to men that all people everywhere should repent" (Acts 17:30 NASB, emphasis added).

Muslims call the period of time before Muhammad the "period of ignorance" (*jahiliyya*) which has given way to God's new era of revelation through Muhammad and the Quran. For most Muslims, this is the point where real history begins—everything before it was corrupted by polytheism and is not worth acknowledging or studying. For Islamic fundamentalists, all contemporary societies have reverted to the immoral paganism and antinomianism of the pre-Islamic heathen civilizations. This reversion to paganism is classified as apostasy and serves as the main legitimization for resistance to what they view as illegitimate, infidel governments. It also justifies the various degrees of violence wielded against those categorized as neo-pagans.

THE CONCEPT OF *JAHILIYYA*

Traditional Islam views the pre-Islamic paganism of Arabia (*jahiliyya*) as a terribly corrupt condition of humanity, without God or his law, lying in the distant past. God intervened by revealing the Quran to Muhammad and instructing him to call all men to the faith of Islam. No one coming after this tremendous event has any excuse for living as a pagan, and so all must be forced to conform to God's law as found in the Sharia.

Fundamentalists have reinterpreted *jahiliyya,* applying it to present day individuals, societies, rulers, and regimes. They assert that it is the present condition of all who do not fully apply Sharia, thus denying God's rule, usurping his authority, and living by man-made laws. As only Sharia-based systems are really legitimate, fundamentalists use the concept of *jahiliyya* to justify the use of force against other Muslims as well as their own governments.

Smashing the False Gods

Islamic fundamentalists accuse secularists of setting up multiple false gods instead of the one true God, and they have a definite iconoclastic streak about them as they seek to eliminate all idols from society. Like Old Testament prophets, Islamic fundamentalists are jealous for God's sole supremacy and are out to destroy all men-made idols (*tawaghit*) that usurp God's place. They see false gods everywhere—the nation state, autonomous man, infidel rulers, science and technology, sexual immorality, and much more. As puritans they rely on Muslim Scriptures as the sole standard for private and public morality, and they see themselves duty-bound to judge evil, separate from it, and enforce morality on all of society and state.

Islamic fundamentalists also see themselves as fighting on God's side in a great cosmic battle against Satan's evil forces. Two incompatible worldviews are struggling for the leadership of humanity: true (fundamentalist) Islam, centered on God and his perfect revelation; and evil secularism, centered on man and his reason. These two worldviews are locked in a constant, deadly battle, and this conflict permeates every level of society.

This battle against *jahiliyya*—understood as any system not based on Quran, Sunna, and Sharia—is seen as a permanent conflict between the Islamic system and all *jahili* systems. As the foundational concepts of the two systems are totally incompatible, Islam cannot coexist with any *jahili* system. Islam means total submission to God and his law, while *jahili* systems are a corrupt deviation from the worship of the one God and his divinely ordained way of life.[104]

Who are the Neo-Pagans?

Radical and mainline movements differ over the application of *jahiliyya* to Muslim societies and states. The central question in these discussions is its extent: Does it apply to society as a whole or only to the regime? Which individuals fall into this category? Does it include the bureaucracy and the military? The clerical establishment? If the entire society, not just the government, is *jahili,* then attacks on civilians (who are effectively apostates) are legitimized—there is no neutral ground.[105]

For the radicals, *jahiliyyja* is the present condition of a society that, by its non-implementation of full Sharia, expresses its revolt against God's sovereignty. All Western societies and international organizations dominated by it are *jahili* as are all contemporary Muslim regimes. The main cause of the present worldwide crisis in morals was this return of humanity to paganism which is equivalent to the dethroning of God from His rightful sovereignty and rule. This crisis is a God-given opportunity for true Islam to step into the breach and lead humanity from the brink of disaster towards a new golden age, as it alone offers the formula for spiritual revival.

According to Qutb, *jahiliyya* is not a pre-Islamic historical era of paganism but an ever present condition of denying God's rule, usurping his authority, and living by man-made laws that enslave humans and engender oppression. *Jahiliyya* is always evil in whatever form it manifests itself, always seeking to crush true Islam. Holy War, *jihad* by the sword, is the weapon for annihilating *jahili* regimes and replacing them with true Islamic systems.[106]

THE CONCEPT OF *TAKFIR*

Islamic fundamentalists feel it is their God-given duty to examine and judge individuals, regimes, societies, and states as to whether they are pagan or truly Muslim. If they are judged to be pagan, they are proclaimed heretical, apostate, infidel, and non-Islamic, deserving of death and subject to Holy War (*jihad*). This semi-legal process of examining, judging, and excommunicating is called *takfir*. It bears certain similarities to the Christian practices of heresy hunting and excommunication. As in Medieval and early Reformation Christianity, so in fundamentalist Islam the heretics are seen as deserving the death sentence unless they recant.

Traditionalist religious scholars recognized the dangers of *takfir* early on, following a period of incessant rebellions in the early Muslim state. These uprisings were usually triggered by various sects claiming that the rulers were not real Muslims but apostates who ought to be resisted and deposed. The *ulama* (clerical experts) therefore ruled that *takfir* should not be used against professing Muslims. The mainline fundamentalist movements, such as the Muslim Brotherhood, follow this tradition and will not pronounce *takfir* on any Muslim, accepting claims of belonging to Islam at face value and leaving the judgment of intentions to God.

Qutb, however, initiated a radical shift by insisting that the first step towards Islamic renewal is the examining and judging of all societies, institutions, and regimes by the criteria of true *tawhid* (the unity of God), *hakimiyya* (God's sovereign governance), and the implementation of Sharia. All who do not fulfill these criteria are to be proclaimed *jahili* by the process of *takfir*—the pronouncement of individuals or communities as apostate, making them legitimate targets for active *jihad*. This reinterpretation of *jahiliyya* and *takfir* unsheathed a tempting weapon for radicals: the possibility of pronouncing all rival individuals, groups, governments, and societies as apostate—thus paving the way for indiscriminate terror. This has been practiced by *al-Jama'a al-Islamiyya* in Egypt and by the Armed Islamic Group (GIA) in Algeria. Their terrorist attacks and massacres have enveloped innocent civilians (including women and children) as well as targeted individuals. According to Qutb, all Western societies, whether Christian, Jewish, or Marxist—along with all contemporary Muslim societies—were denounced as *jahili*. No truly Islamic state was said to exist in the world today.[107]

According to the radicals, the failure to implement Sharia in any state makes that state a *jahili* state under *takfir*. This results in a legal obligation on all true Muslims to wage Holy War (*jihad*) against it. Movements such as *al-Jihad* in Egypt claimed that gradualist attempts at reform were un-Quranic. They viewed most regimes in Muslim countries as in a state of *jahiliyya* resembling the pagan pre-Islamic era. However, for contemporary radicals modern *jahiliyya* is far worse than its original model as it includes the rejection of the message of Islam: "It is not a *jahiliyya* of ignorance, but a *jahiliyya* of conscious rejection."[108]

The Egyptian *Takfir wal-Hijra* group declared both regime and society in Egypt as *jahili* and under *takfir*.[109] They went so far as to state that all Islamic communities since Muhammad and the early righteous Caliphs had been *jahili*. All traditions that followed Quran and Sunna, including the four legal schools of Islam, were mere traditions of men and therefore *jahili*. Was not the Quran given in plain Arabic that is absolutely clear for every reader? Consequently, they saw no need for *imams* to establish legal schools. By closing the door of personal interpretation (*ijtihad*), these scholars had turned themselves into *tawaghit* (pagan idols) and acted as false mediators between God and the believer.[110]

On the other hand, Faraj, the founder of *al-Jihad*, did not see all of society as *jahili*. Neither did he reject the four *madhabs* (legal schools). Rather, he taught that Muslim societies consist of a mixture of true Muslims and *jahilis*. However, while societies are *intermixed*, the rulers are all *jahili* because, while claiming to be Islamic, they rule according to their own whims.[111]

8

"Let the High Praises of God be in Their Mouths,
and a Double-Edged Sword in Their Hand,
To Execute Vengeance on the Nations"[112]

THE CONCEPT OF JIHAD

INTRODUCTION

The rhetoric of warfare is prominent in most religions. Following eras in which Holy War (Crusade) was taken as a literal obligation, Christianity now stresses the symbolic and spiritual aspects of warfare terminology. For example, there is a real moral battle being fought in the realms of personal spiritual and moral development, as well as in the sphere of ideas, worldviews, and ideologies.[113] However, the rhetoric around this theme of warfare can be manipulated to mobilize followers into activism, evoking historical precedents and easily blurring the distinctions between the literal and the spiritual. Terms such as Crusade and Holy War can be reinterpreted to legitimize violent struggle in contexts where it is claimed that the utopian end justifies the violent means. Fairly recently Orthodox Christians in the former Yugoslavia used this kind of Holy War rhetoric to justify their battles against the Muslims among them.

In Islam, *jihad* is a basic concept taught by Muhammad and accepted as a central religious duty which has been invoked innumerable times in Muslim history to justify wars against identified enemies. *Jihad* is also a very popular concept in Islamic heroic folklore and myth and arouses huge emotional sympathies among all Muslim populations. Traditional Islam allowed only competent clerics to declare *jihad* after due deliberation, and it was hedged about by elaborate conditions in order to limit its misuse. In contrast, Islamic fundamentalists have popularized *jihad* as an effective tool to be used against all enemies in their struggle for an Islamic state, with lay leaders arrogating to themselves the authority to issue declarations of *jihad*. Some indeed turn it into a sixth pillar of Islam—the missing or forgotten obligation.

For many Muslims, *jihad* also means the continuous struggle against all evil that stands in God's way, both internally within each person and externally within society and state. Though it can take many forms, including campaigns to improve legislation or to fight poverty and disease, right from Muhammad's time it has also signified Holy War to deter political aggression or defend the Muslim community. It was also interpreted early on to imply the duty of every Muslim and of all true Muslim communities to wage a continuous war against unbelievers—individuals, groups, societies, regimes, and states—until they submit to Islamic rule. This urge for political domination of the world remains an inbuilt reflex in much of Islam to this day.

While accepting the individual internal struggle as important, many Islamic fundamentalists see *jihad* as primarily an external struggle against evil and enemies in society or as a means for propagating a true Islamic Sharia system around the world. The question is whether the goal is to be achieved by a peaceful struggle using Islamic mission (*da'wa*) or by the use of force. Radicals go beyond the concepts of improving society and defending Muslim states against aggressors to include aggressive violent action aimed at taking over power in the state and, ultimately, in the whole world. They justify attacks on *jahili* states, Muslim and non-Muslim, by declaring that all such states belong to the camp of war (*dar-al-harb*) with which true Islam can never have permanent peace since it has been ordered by God to impose the Islamic system on the whole world by force.

JIHAD AS A REVOLUTIONARY STRUGGLE

Extremists advocating the use of force have carried Qutb's radical reinterpretations of *jahiliyya, hakimiyya, takfir,* and *jihad* to their logical conclusion. These groups see themselves as the vanguard of true Islam in its struggle to destroy *jahiliyya* and establish a renewed universal Caliphate that will fully implement Sharia. The necessary first step towards this ultimate goal is the violent take-over of power in individual Muslim states.

Qutb, while accepting that *jihad* had defensive aspects, stressed its offensive nature for the expansion of true Islam. As *jahiliyya* is always evil in any form it manifests itself, *jihad* by force (*bil saif*) must be used against it. God has provided Islam with *jihad* as the means of subjugating all political authorities worldwide to his religion. This is especially true of *jahili* regimes that must be annihilated and replaced by Islamic systems. The goal of *jihad* by force is to free all people from enslavement to tyrants so that they might serve God alone. With the establishment of a utopian Islamic society that operates according to God's will, all will be free, all will be equally slaves to God, legal and social justice will be practiced, and greed and usury eliminated.[114]

Mawdudi explains *jihad* as the revolutionary struggle to establish God's just order on earth in an equitable society with an Islamic ideology. It is the duty of true believers to enforce Allah's law and annihilate all oppression, immorality, arrogance, and exploitation by force of arms. Because evil systems flourish and no pious order can ever be established under evil government, the Islamic party has no option but to wrest the authority of government from wicked hands and transfer it to the hands of true Muslims.[115]

Radicals view *jihad* as aggressive and imperative. The Egyptian *Takfir wal Hijra* stated that Muhammad had ordered Muslims to fight all people until they all convert, pray, and pay *zakat* (obligatory religious tax). This ultimate goal has never yet been achieved in history. *Takfir* wanted first to establish its rule over Egypt and then issue a call to all humanity to join Islam and submit to Sharia. Those who reject the call must be fought against until they submit. The Islamic state will then become the third superpower of the world, gradually extending its dominion over the entire earth.[116]

Faraj of *al-Jihad* declared the regime in Egypt—including all its employees—as *jahili* and under *takfir* and declared *jihad* against them as justified and imperative. *Jihad* by the sword was God's solution to the problem of dealing with unbelievers and apostate rulers, and it is also the suppressed sixth pillar of Islam (the forgotten obligation), the main religious duty of true Muslims that must be given top priority. True Islam means continuous *jihad* against all pagan rulers and states even if they call themselves Muslims. There was no excuse for postponing the inevitable violent confrontation. Killing true Muslims employed by the regime was justified by referring to Muhammad's example and the work of famous commentators. So was the infiltration of the enemy camp and the use of deception in overthrowing the regime. Faraj dealt with various excuses put forward for postponing active *jihad* or interpreting it as defensive or non-violent and concluded that they were all wrong and that active, violent, and immediate *jihad* is the only God-given strategy for achieving an Islamic state.[117]

Other radicals also agree that *jihad* must be waged against unbelievers at all times and places.[118] It is the means by which to establish the Caliphate, after removing the infidel rulers who have usurped God's position, and to establish God's law as supreme. *Jihad* is an obligation on all Muslims and it is an unforgivable crime to abandon it.[119]

Ali Shariati in the Shia camp argued that *jihad* as revolution was the only alternative left for effecting change. For Shariati, the main tool for mobilizing Muslim societies was Islamic ideology which replaces the fatalistic "is" with the utopian "ought to be." This dialectical tension would catalyze Muslims to overthrow the unbearable present and establish utopia. Similar to liberation theology teaching, Shariati saw Islam as a revolutionary ideology that is permitted to use force because it sides with the oppressed and is biased towards the poor. In true Islam "God is the God of the oppressed" and the "God of the deprived." Islamic ideology is the panacea for all problems of Muslim societies because it combines a scientific and deterministic philosophy of history with a positive humanism and with the belief in the inevitable victory of the oppressed.[120]

HISTORICAL DEVELOPMENTS

Classical Islam developed partly in response to the many violent rebellions against state authority by groups using *takfir* as their justification. The clerics ruled that it must not be used against professing Muslims. The Wahhabis of Arabia were the first to reintroduce the sectarian concept of *takfir* into their doctrinal worldview. Muhammad Ibn 'Abd al-Wahhab, founder of the Wahhabi movement, used *takfir* against both non-Muslims and Muslims he identified as infidels. He was also the first to expand the concept of *jahiliyya* to include Muslim societies of his time that had departed from the pure path of Quran and Sunna by venerating saints and their tombs.[121] Designating Muslims as *jahilis* and *kafirs* (infidels and unbelievers) opened the way for proclaiming *jihad* against them.[122] Early Wahhabism influenced contemporary fundamentalist movements in Egypt via Rashid Rida who accepted many of their ideas in formulating the contemporary *salafi* worldview (the call for a return to the practices of Muhammad and the first generation of Muslims).

The Saudi government has encouraged and financed modern Wahhabi movements across the Muslim world and sponsored a wide variety of radical Islamist movements abroad, thus spreading these concepts in contemporary Muslim societies. Since the 1950s, when Saudi Arabia supported Egyptian fundamentalists against the Arab nationalist regime of Egyptian President Gamal Abdel Nasser, there has been a process of cross-fertilization between Wahhabism and contemporary fundamentalism. Radical Saudi opposition figures, such as Usama bin-Laden, currently carry on this integrated Wahhabi-fundamentalist legacy.[123] The Afghan *jihad* against the Soviets saw these concepts radicalize Pakistani and Afghani traditional reform movements of the Deobandi School (like *Jamiat-e Ulema-i Islam*) which eventually gave birth to the Taliban movement.[124]

'Abdullah 'Azzam (1941-1989), a prominent Palestinian *jihad* fighter in Afghanistan and considered by many to be bin-Laden's mentor, saw *jihad* as the greatest religious obligation. It is God's ordained method for establishing Islam in the world.[125] Only the ill, the crippled, children, women who cannot emigrate, and the aged are excused from this duty, which is an act of communal worship of God conducted under a recognized leader.[126]

Following Faraj, 'Azzam claimed that this obligation has been forgotten, and its neglect is the cause of contemporary Muslim humiliation. When not under direct attack by unbelievers, *jihad* is a communal obligation (*fard kifaya*) undertaken by the government and armed forces of the Islamic state and fulfilled by the Imam sending out an army at least once a year "to terrorize the enemies of Allah." However, when infidels occupy Muslim land, *jihad* becomes a compulsory individual obligation on every single Muslim (*fard 'ayn*) and remains so until the liberation of the last occupied piece of Muslim land. 'Azzam offers quotes from the four legal schools to support this view. As infidels today occupy Muslim lands in Palestine, Afghanistan, Kashmir, and many other places, it is clear that the obligation is a personal one on all Muslims.[127]

'Azzam also calls for Muslims to give up narrow nationalism and let their vision extend beyond national borders that have been established by imperialist unbelievers. He rejects all arguments against immediate *jihad*, such as the lack of a qualified *Amir* (princely leader), internal squabbles among Muslims, or the lack of manpower. Nothing annuls the obligation of fighting in the defense of Muslim lands. Indeed, the conduction of *jihad* is part of the process of uniting Muslims and establishing a real Caliphate.[128]

Usama bin-Laden does not theorize about *jihad* but simply claims that it has always been part of Islam, instituted for the repelling of infidel invaders. The stationing of Western military bases on the soil of Muslim states constitutes an occupation by infidels, a clear cause for *jihad*.[129] In his notorious "Ladinese Epistle" in which he declared *jihad* against America, he bases himself on the medieval commentator Ibn-Taymiyya who stressed the priority of dealing with the "greater kufr" before dealing with other, lesser *kufrs,* based on the principle of necessity. It is a religious duty to repel the greatest danger first even if it means ignoring smaller enemies for a while. He identifies the greater *kufr* as America because of its occupation of the Arabian Peninsula and its support of Israel.[130]

SHIFT TO INTERNATIONALISM

In the 1970s and 1980s, most radical Islamic groups tended to focus their violent activities on destabilizing and destroying the infidel regimes in their own states, following the injunction of fighting the enemies at hand before dealing with enemies further away. The 1990s saw a shift due to the catalytic effect of the Afghan war against the Soviet occupation. Thousands of volunteers from across the Muslim world joined the *jihad* against the Soviets, and a measure of cooperation was forged between the widely divergent groups in spite of many internal conflicts.[131] Their victory over the Soviet superpower coupled with the interchange of ideas and the links forged between groups helped internationalize the movement.

Afghan veterans returning home after the Soviet withdrawal radicalized local fundamentalist groups and caused a marked increase in violence in their home countries, especially in Algeria and Egypt. Others found new sponsors and moved to other regions where they believed infidels were attacking Muslim communities such as Kashmir, Bosnia, Chechnya, Kosovo, and the Philippines. They have also been instrumental in radicalizing local fundamentalist groups and intensifying local conflicts in Indonesia and sub-Saharan Africa.[132]

Another development of the 1990s was the relocation of the headquarters of many radical movements from their countries of origin to Western nations because of severe repression in their home countries. Many leaders and activists went into exile to Western Europe, the United States, and Canada where they utilized the relative freedom of operation granted them in the secular-liberal democracies to set up bases and networks. From the West they could more effectively oversee their networks, link up with each other, and propagate their doctrines back into their home countries using the globalizing technologies of fax, e-mail, and the world-wide-web, while recruiting new members in the Western Muslim communities and raising finances for increased activities.[133]

The Gulf War further radicalized these groups by underlining their views that the West still wanted to re-colonize Muslim states. They were especially enraged by the permanent stationing of American troops in Saudi Arabia. The presence of infidel soldiers polluting the Holy Land of the two holy shrines was seen as an aggressive act aimed at dominating the Muslim heartland.

The United States thus became the enemy near at hand and the major focus of attention for groups like *al-Jihad* and *al-Jama'a al-Islamiyya*. Usama bin-Laden's *al-Qa'ida* was in the forefront of those who encouraged interaction and networking among all such movements around the world, preparing for assaults that would really hurt and humiliate America. Petty squabbles and opposition to corrupt regimes in Muslim lands became secondary in light of this *jihad* against the *greater kufr*. The results of this shift have now been seen in the bombings of the American embassies in Nairobi and Dar al-Salaam and in the dramatic attacks on the Twin Towers in New York using hijacked civilian planes.

Where Does Usama Bin-Laden Fit In?

Bin-Laden is not an impassioned revolutionary radical like Qutb or Shariati, seeking social justice for the poor and oppressed.

Nor is he the product of harassment, imprisonment, or torture at the hand of Muslim regimes as are the leaders of the Egyptian *jihad* and *jama'a* groups. Rather, bin-Laden is a product of traditional Saudi Wahhabism, enjoying riches and a privileged position until his radicalization in the Afghan wars. However, his close association with radical, ideological, Egyptian fundamentalist groups such as *al-jihad* has clearly impacted his ideology.

Bin-Laden does not mention the concepts of *jahiliyya* and *takfir* in his interviews, *fatwas*, and statements. He focuses on *jihad*, as understood by the more traditionalist clerics—a defensive struggle against enemies who attack and occupy Muslim lands. It was not Qutb's theories and reinterpretations that mobilized him but the Soviet invasion of Muslim Afghanistan and the stationing of American troops in Saudi-Arabia. His focus is not on replacing the corrupt Saudi regime (though he does label it as an American stooge whose turn will eventually come) but on fighting the external foes of Islam whoever they may be.[134]

He is characterized by a pan-Islamic ideology that does not recognize internal divisions in the Muslim *umma* and a sense of grievance at the worldwide weakness of Muslims and their humiliation at the hands of the West. His capabilities in administration and technical matters as well as his charisma and motivating power and ability to form alliances across a wide spectrum of ideologies, have placed him in the forefront of radical Islamists using terror to further their cause. He is not a shadowy secretive figure like other leaders of radical groups but rather courts publicity, giving interviews and appearing on videos and TV programs. The staggering magnitude of his exploits in terms of victims and destruction and his gift for public relations have made him the darling of Muslim masses worldwide, appealing to their popular views of *jihad*, articulating their sense of wounded pride and wish for revenge, and identifying a highly visible scapegoat, the United States, as the root of all evil and corruption.

THE SWORD OF GOD

Radical Islamic fundamentalists happily assume the role of God's weapon of wrath against his unbelieving, rebellious, and immoral enemies at this stage of world history. Many have eschatological tendencies of seeing themselves part of God's end-time scenario, preparing the way for the promised deliverer (*mahdi*) who will set up God's kingdom of justice and peace. Supported by Quranic and Hadith texts about the terrible events of the last days, they assume that the indiscriminate terrorism they are engaged in is part of God's cleansing fire of wrath poured on a rebellious humanity. Like the puritans in Reformation Europe, they have no compunctions in forcing their religious worldview on society and state, severely punishing all who would oppose or disagree. Great inner conviction and fanatical zeal are characteristics of all fundamentalist Islamic groups.

ISLAM AND WORLD DOMINION

Just as many Christians work towards the winning of the world for Christ, so many Muslims dream of winning the world for Islam. However, the Muslim vision is far more focused on political power than on individual conversion, as for most Muslims there is no division between religion and politics. Muslim movements and governments often see fundamentalists as the front troops in this laudable drive to politically dominate the world, which explains why the regimes in Saudi Arabia, Iran, Pakistan, and other Muslim states have so energetically supported *jihad* organizations across the world. Various Muslim fundamentalist groups have actually developed a many-pronged, long-term strategy to achieve this ultimate goal. Some of the strands in this strategy are:

The Islamization of Knowledge

This is very much an elite undertaking by academics and professionals. Academic institutions and think tanks founded in the West and funded by rich Muslim states and individuals aim to influence Western science and shift it in the direction of an integration of all human knowledge into one Islamic system based on *tawhid* and Sharia.

Active Missionary Activity (*da'wa*)

Rich oil states and wealthy Muslim businessmen fund missionaries, a vast publishing endeavor, and the founding of mosques, madrassas, and other Muslim institutions in the non-Muslim world.

A Demographic Victory

The population explosion in Muslim societies coupled to the increasing number of Muslims emigrating to the West are viewed as being acts of God's providence, tilting the balance decisively in favor of Islam. Islam can thus be depicted as the fastest growing religion in the world, this being understood as a sure sign of God's favor.

The Full Islamization of Muslim-Majority States

This includes destabilizing secular regimes in Muslim states and replacing them with Islamic state systems based on Sharia. Iran, Sudan, and the Taliban in Afghanistan are examples of countries where this has already happened. Algeria and Egypt are examples of countries where violent attempts have so far been thwarted, but the danger remains.

The Introduction of Sharia Law

There is a widespread and often violent agitation for this in countries with large Muslim minorities, especially in the Third World (Nigeria is an example). Once introduced, Sharia ensures the dominance of Islam over the non-Muslim inhabitants of these societies who quickly lose their equal status and become second-rate citizens in their own countries.

Infiltration of Western Societies

This works especially well in societies that harbor relatively large Muslim minorities. The strategy is to infiltrate the educational, academic, and economic systems as well as the power centers and political lobbies in order to impact them in favor of Islam.

Destabilizing the Border Areas of Islam

This is carried out mainly by radical fundamentalist movements but often supported by interested neighboring states that supply safe havens, funds, and recruits. Kashmir is one obvious example. The Philippines is another. Islamic states like Sudan pursue their own version of the Islamization and the ethnic cleansing of their non-Muslim minorities. A similar movement is evident in Indonesia where radical groups have been attacking Christian villages, massacring some of their inhabitants and forcefully converting others, causing a flood of internal refugees in their drive to establish Muslim superiority in all regions of Indonesia. The call for *jihad* in these border areas results in much emotional support across the Muslim world and in volunteers and finance pouring in to support the holy cause. The borders of unbelief are thus constantly being rolled back in favor of Islam.

9

"Let Me Die with the Philistines!"[135]

MARTYRDOM AND SUICIDE MISSIONS

INTRODUCTION

Fascination with death, bloodshed, and suicide is a human condition not limited to any one ideology, religion, society, or time. The demons of death and evil lurk close to the surface of all human societies at all times. All it usually takes is the right crisis, social upheaval, war, spiritual or moral decline, frustration, despair-producing alienation, or evil charismatic leader—and they burst into the open and wreak havoc. Of course, the root cause from an evangelical point of view is the depraved and sinful nature of all humans, necessitating God's redeeming intervention through the cross of Christ. Sin is present in all societies, though it expresses itself differently in different times and contexts.

Islamic fundamentalists do not hold a monopoly on violence, terrorism, or suicide bombings. History reveals that, since ancient times, many groups and societies have fallen prey to a fascination with death expressed through killing frenzies, indiscriminate bloodshed, a collective death wish, or a tendency toward suicide. Themes of sacrifice and bloodshed for the holy cause typify all human conflicts and often spin out of control when pushed beyond all other considerations.

Indiscriminate bloodshed has long been a mark of secular ideological revolutions. It characterized the French Revolution (state terror, the guillotine), the Russian Bolshevik Revolution, and a wide variety of anarchist and nihilist movements throughout Europe. Death, either by killing others or killing oneself, was part of the "end justifies the means" syndrome that marked Fascism and Nazism as well as Marxism and Maoism. The Holocaust and the Gulag, Stalin's terror, the Maoist Shining Path guerrillas of Peru, and the Killing Fields of Cambodia all mark the willingness of groups with secular revolutionary ideologies to shed innocent blood on a massive scale as a catalyst for achieving their aims. Nation states also tend to use indiscriminate violence either to suppress internal dissent or to war against external enemies.

Ethnic conflicts and national liberation movements also gravitate toward indiscriminate bloodshed. The Rwandan genocide of Tutsis by Hutus is one recent example, and the civil war in Lebanon with its countless atrocities committed by the various sectarian groups against each other is another. Until recently, the Sri Lankan Tamil Tigers held the worldwide record for the number of suicide bombings undertaken by any one movement (that distinction is now held by Palestinian suicide bombers). Ethnic cleansing in the former Yugoslavia, atrocities in Chechnya, killings and bombings by terrorist groups like the IRA in Britain, the Basque ETA, and the Kurdish PKK in Turkey all reveal that national or ethnic liberation movements are only too happy to slaughter civilians and sacrifice themselves in suicidal efforts for the cause.

Finally, this fascination with death is a characteristic of certain religious trends, both mainline and sectarian. While mainline religions tend to stress the holiness of all life as given by God, there are times when a morbid preoccupation with death seems to predominate, as when religious goals can be construed to justify all means. Recent events in Gujarat, India, have again shown the ease with which "religious" people can be manipulated to go off on killing sprees. Hatred of unbelievers (or of other-believers) can easily be fanned by religious leaders into a frenzy of slaughter. Whether in *jihad*, the Crusades, the Inquisition, the persecution of heretics, or the utopian search for a millennial kingdom, bloodshed, martyrdom, and suicide can easily become normal and accepted.

At this moment in history, following the fall of the Soviet Union and the demise of communism, it is the turn of Islamist extremists to succumb to the "fascination with death" syndrome and the indiscriminate-bloodshed virus. Examples are everywhere, from the GIA slaughter of civilians in Algeria, Hizbullah and Hamas suicide bombers in Lebanon and Israel, and the various *jihad*-terrorist groups operating in Kashmir, the Philippines, and Indonesia, to the work of Usama bin-Laden and his *al-Qa'ida* group in New York, Washington, D.C., and around the world. Bin-Ladin stands in a long line of Islamic extremists who have invoked religion to justify indiscriminate slaughter, even motivating believers to commit suicide in the process. Radical Islamic fundamentalist groups have a millenarian ideology whose goal is to usher in God's kingdom on earth. The violence they unleash is seen as part of God's righteous wrath and judgment on the evils of humanity.

HONOR AND SHAME AS MOTIVATORS

"Without shedding blood no degradation and branding can be removed from the forehead... Death is better than humiliation! Some scandals and shame will never be otherwise eradicated."[136]

Honor and shame are not exclusively Muslim themes. They are very important in Japanese culture as well, and much of Japan's behavior during and following WWII is linked to the supreme importance of these themes to the Japanese. To divert the shame of imminent defeat, many young Japanese pilots joined in Kamikaze suicide attacks on allied targets, and several high commanders of the Japanese armed forces committed *hara kiri* to atone for the shame of surrender. Even the rise to power of the Nazi party in Germany during the 1930s was rooted in a deeply-felt humiliation carried by many Germans from their defeat in WWI.

However, the honor and shame theme is an especially important component of Muslim societies. This fact is borne out by the continued widespread incidence of honor killings in Muslim states in which women suspected of immorality are killed by their male relatives. The legal systems and judiciary of these states take a lenient view of such murders because they are seen as a legitimate means of restoring honor to the affected families. In most Muslim societies it is still true that only blood can really wipe out shame and humiliation. The greater the shame, the greater the bloodshed needed to wipe it out: ". . . the only way to be freed from humiliation is by the sword. . . ."[137]

Muslims, and especially Arabs, feel humiliated and shamed by the West, a feeling strengthened by the incessant propaganda of governments happy to blame others for their own failures. They sense they have been dominated, exploited, manipulated, and betrayed by it. As a result, there is much admiration throughout the Muslim world for bin-Laden. The attacks of September 11, 2001, are seen as just retribution and revenge for Muslim humiliations. Radicals have used the honor/shame complex to arouse sympathy for their goals and methods. The greatest humiliation bin-Laden mentions in his statements is the abolition of the Caliphate by Attaturk in 1924, followed by the Jewish takeover of Palestine and Jerusalem, the continued bombing of and sanctions against Iraq, and finally the stationing of American infidel troops in Saudi Arabia, thus polluting the Holy Land of the two shrines.[138]

FASCINATION WITH DEATH

Though passive martyrdom was eagerly sought and glorified in early Christianity, modern Christianity (including evangelicalism) views it only as a last resort. Holy War (Crusade), in turn, has come to be understood mainly in its spiritual and symbolic sense. The suicide motif appears only on the millenarian fringes with such groups as the People's Temple in Jonestown, Guyana, and the followers of David Koresh in Waco, Texas.

Holy War (*jihad*) and martyrdom (*istishhad*) have always been popular motives in Islam, evoking deep emotions of identification and sympathy. They are based on Quranic and Hadith texts that give them legitimacy across the ages. (They can, of course, be easily manipulated to bring terror and destruction against any identified enemy; but this often proves dangerous as, once unleashed, they can easily boomerang back on those who first unleashed them, often harming unexpected new victims in the process.) Modern Islamic fundamentalists have revived these concepts in their literalist sense, using martyrdom as a potent weapon in the arsenal of *jihad*. More alarming has been their revival of suicide attacks as a legitimate form of martyrdom. Aggressive martyrdom is now being encouraged and glorified by Islamic fundamentalists and its rewards in Paradise are strongly stressed as blandishments for new recruits. Radicals have revived sectarian Islamic traditions of suicide-killings as a legitimate weapon in their contemporary *jihad*.[139] This is especially true of Shia fundamentalist[140] but has also motivated Sunni groups to encourage and organize acts of violent martyrdom.[141]

Religious symbolism is used in selecting the targets of Islamic terrorism to cause maximum psychological trauma to the enemy. Radicals see Western societies as crippled by atheism, materialism, and secularism that have created a morbid fear of death as the greatest possible evil among their populations. True Muslims, on the other hand, have no fear of death, as they know God has predetermined their destiny and will reward their sacrifice—hence the efficiency of suicide bombings to strike terror into the heart of Western society.[142]

Martyrdom is seen as a sure way to God's favor, and it is assumed that because of it He will grant success to the movement. As human sacrifice of self and others becomes acceptable, innocent victims become necessary to feed the vicious circle. Suicide bombers undergo ritual ceremonies of dedication before going out on their missions. No pity is felt for innocent victims, who in some cases (Algeria) have their throats slit as sheep to the slaughter, offered up to God as sacrifices in the righteous cause. The victims propitiate God's wrath, and the martyrs please God and receive divine rewards. A recent example is the four-page Arabic document found in the luggage and cars of the perpetrators of the September 11, 2001, plane hijackings. Among other things, it states:

If God grants you a slaughter, you should perform it
as an offering on behalf of your father and mother,
for they are owed by you.[143]

Passengers killed in the hijackings and plane crashes are viewed as ritual sacrifices provided by God to the hijackers to be offered up to him in an act of worship.[144]

Shari'ati laid great stress on martyrdom as a revolutionary weapon. Its utility lies in its being an integral part of Shia ideology motivating men to become the martyrs who are the heartbeat of history. The martyrdom of Hussein, Muhammad's grandson and a role model for Shia Muslims, is the great paradigm: a protest against tyranny and a witness to the true values of Islam, guaranteeing that faith would survive. Martyrdom is seen as a legitimate, deliberate choice that will strengthen future generations while shaming the evil powers of the enemy. It is a true *jihad* that guarantees honor, faith, and the future of the powerless. It transforms the Shia from being passive "guardians of the cemeteries" to active followers of Ali and Hussein, fighting for truth on every front. Shari'ati argues that when false religion is victorious, when all avenues of protest are closed, and when potential revolutionaries are bribed, co-opted, or killed, then Hussein's model teaches man to be a martyr and by his death to become a witness to the truth and a shaker of the evil empire: "It is an invitation to all ages and generations that if you cannot kill, die."[145] The utility of the martyr motive to the revolution was later demonstrated by the myriads of idealistic young Iranians who found their death on the killing fields of the Iraq-Iran war when volunteering for duty as human assault waves or living land-mine detonators.

Khomeini, who had stated as early as 1942 that the aim of

Islamic *jihad* is to conquer the whole world,[146] repeatedly stressed the centrality of martyrdom to Islam, declaring that "Islam grew with blood" and that Muslims have no fear of death, as the reward in the afterlife is so sublime.[147]

Once accepted as legitimate, radicals utilized the notions of martyrdom and self-sacrifice through suicide bombings as efficient weapons against more powerful enemies. Members of *Hizbullah* were the first to use it in Lebanon against the American, French, and Israeli troops starting in 1983, emulating the actions of Iranian Revolutionary Guard shock troops in the war against Iraq. Various Shia clerics offered theological justifications, although suicide is generally forbidden in Islam.

The legitimacy of martyrdom and suicide missions was later adopted by Sunni radicals (as demonstrated by the Sunni Palestinian Hamas and Jihad suicide bombings in Israel), and it has become an important weapon in their efforts to sabotage the Israeli-Palestinian Oslo Peace process. Sunni *al-Qa'ida* members were also responsible for the suicidal attacks on the World Trade Center in New York.

Traditional Islam forbids suicide, stressing that it is not part of the Sharia teaching on *jihad* and is therefore a major sin. In addition, it forbids the killing of non-combatants, women, children, and the elderly.[148] However, though most radicals agree that suicide as such is a major sin forbidden in Islam, they use Quranic verses, Hadith narratives, and cases from early Islamic history to prove that the voluntary sacrifice of oneself in the cause of Islam—with the goal of defending Muslims and hurting their enemies—is not considered suicide but is a legitimate fight to the death.[149] Others see it as martyrdom, which is different from suicide and legitimate in Islam as a form of fulfilling the individual duty of *jihad*. Sheikh Yusuf al-Qaradawi (Head of the Department of Sunna Studies at the University of Qatar, a prominent Egyptian cleric and scholar, and considered a moderate Muslim Brotherhood member) argues that suicide bombings have nothing to do with suicide. Rather, they are "heroic operations of martyrdom, the supreme form of Jihad for the sake of Allah, and a type of terrorism that is allowed by the Shari'a."[150]

In these discussions the intent behind the attempt is all-important. All agree that someone attempting to end his life for personal reasons is committing a forbidden act of suicide. Muhammad Sayyed Tantawi, Sheikh of al-Azhar, argues that suicide operations are to be regarded as martyrdom if the intention is to kill enemy soldiers but not women or children. Al-Qaradawi argued that they are legal even if women and children are killed because Israeli society is militaristic by nature and women serve in its army. However, children and the elderly should not be targeted, though if they are killed accidentally this can be excused by the principle of necessity. A group of al-Azhar scholars published a *fatwa* supporting suicide attacks in which people sacrifice themselves to protect the rights, honor, and land of Muslims.[151]

Following the attack on the Twin Towers, the Grand Mufti of Saudi Arabia, Sheikh Abdul Aziz ibn-Abdullah ibn-Muhammad Al el Sheikh, issued a statement that condemned the act as criminal on the grounds that Islam forbids hijacking of planes, the terrorizing of innocent people, and the shedding of blood. This is representative of many regime scholars issuing statements justifying their government's support of the United States. However, he did not touch on the question of martyrdom or suicide—a significant omission.[152] At the same time, the reaction of the masses on the streets of most large Muslim cities around the world showed that many were in clear sympathy with the suicide bombers.

Fundamentalist clerics stress that the martyr does not even feel the pain of death. All his sins are forgiven, he has guaranteed immediate access into paradise, and he has the right to intercede for his family to enter heaven. "From the moment his blood is spilled, he does not feel the pain of his wounds and he is forgiven for all of his sins; he sees his seat in paradise; he is saved from the torment of the grave; he is saved from the great horror of Judgment Day; he marries the 'black-eyed' *houris*; he intercedes successfully with God for 70 of his family members; and he gains the crown of honor, the precious stone of which is better than this entire world."[153]

The concept of being a martyr (*shahid*) signifies a life sacrificed for a cause and an act of "bearing witness" to the world, proving the cause worthy of the ultimate sacrifice. A martyr's death in God's way and in his service is the best death in Islam. Celebrations of martyrdom demonstrate respect and love for the one who has made the ultimate sacrifice. The pure motive of the martyrs is a threat and challenge to the enemy. The human bomb's willingness to face death is proof of his faith in his Lord that overcomes the fear of death, of the enemies, and of what they can do to him. The martyr is not afraid of death because he loves God, is glad to meet his creator, and knows the hereafter is far better than this world. Overcoming the fear of death is an act of courage, and the idea of redemption through death is universal. Human bombs are seen as good Muslims who are more devoted to the cause of justice than they are to life.[154]

10

"Looking for and Hastening the Coming of the Day of God"[155]

MESSIANISM AND MILLENNIALISM

INTRODUCTION

"End-time" scenarios have always played an important role in the Christian—and especially evangelical—worldview. The culmination of all things in Christ and the destruction of God's enemies bring final resolution to the long and complex story of human history on the earth. In the same vein, classical Islamic eschatology predicts a period of great cosmic conflict preceding the final resurrection and judgment. This tribulation period is characterized by natural catastrophes as well as terrible wars. An Antichrist figure (*al-dajjal*) appears who causes corruption all over the world for a limited period of time, deceiving many by his miracles and false teachings. A heaven-sent savior, the *mahdi,* then appears to fight the forces of Satan, restore Islam to its original perfection and glory, and set up God's kingdom on earth.[156]

Muslims in all traditions accept the *mahdi* narratives and wait for the messianic deliverer. The *mahdi* concept is especially important for the Shia, who believe that their last Imam did not die but is now in a supernatural state of occultation (the Hidden Imam) from which he will visibly return as the *mahdi* to initiate a period of universal peace, prosperity, and justice in which all humanity will accept Islam. In the meantime, believers undergo a season of trials and testing in which they are called to watch for the "signs of the times" as revealed in the apocalyptic prophecies.

Self-proclaimed *mahdis* have emerged all over the Muslim world throughout its history, posing a danger to established rulers who have tended to suppress them for causing *fitna* (confusion, disorder).[157] Self-proclaimed *mahdis* also led resistance movements to Western imperialism in the nineteenth century, one example being the Sudanese Muhammad Ahmad ibn-'Abd Allah who set up an independent Sharia state (1882–1898). The concept of *Mahdism* has brought great mobilizing power to Muslims of all times, especially during times of crisis and weakness.

Islamic fundamentalists in general accept the traditional teachings of their religion on the end times, and their concepts of eschatology play an important part in their worldview. They see themselves engaged in the final battle of the end times where it is important to identify enemies and practice both separatism and active involvement in world affairs.[158]

While eschatology might play a lesser part among fundamentalist Islamists than among evangelical Christians (especially of the premillennial-dispensationalist persuasion), most accept the traditional Sunni or Shia eschatological teachings on the signs of the end times: the appearance of the Antichrist (*al-dajjal*) and the coming of the *mahdi* (or the return of the Hidden *Imam*) to set up a righteous rule on earth.[159] However, some groups are more heavily influenced by Islamic eschatology and perceive their activities as part of the end-time scenario.

RADICALS AND ESCHATOLOGY

Some radicals, while accepting eschatological and messianic themes, stress the duty of true believers to be actively engaged in establishing the Islamic state without waiting for the *mahdi*. 'Abd al-Salam Faraj accepted the traditions of the *mahdi* who will reveal himself at the end of time and establish justice in the whole world. This, however, should not result in passivity. Rather, true Muslims are duty bound to actively fulfill God's original mandate of spreading Islam to the whole world before the end-time appearance of the *mahdi*. Lack of messianic leadership is no excuse for postponing the struggle, as leadership in the meantime can be given to the best Muslim in the community.[160]

Other radical groups are more heavily influenced by eschatology and *mahdism,* viewing their activities as part of the end-time scenario. Eschatology and millenarianism play an important part in the worldview of these groups, encouraging separatism, helping them identify enemies, and justifying conspiracy theories and violence.[161]

The appearance of a charismatic *mahdist* leader figure is often the catalyst for such phenomena. Shukri Mustafa, a disciple of Sayyid Qutb, founded *Takfir wal-Hijra* in Egypt as a *mahdist* movement with an eschatological worldview similar to Christian premillennialism. The world was nearing its end as indicated by the signs of disbelief, oppression, immorality, famine, wars, earthquakes, and hurricanes. Mustafa, the charismatic leader, was the promised *mahdi* who would found the new Muslim community, conquer the world, and usher in God's final reign on earth.[162]

In Saudi Arabia, Jahaymin al-'Utaybi (1943-1979), a strict *Wahhabi* disillusioned by the profligate lifestyle of the royal family, led a failed revolt against the Saudi regime in 1979 proclaiming a friend of his, Muhammad ibn-'Abd Allah al-Qahtani, as the *mahdi*. Al-Qahtani's *mahdi* status had been revealed in dreams to his wife and sister and coincided with the beginning of the fifteenth Islamic century. His followers claimed that al-Qahtani fulfilled the Hadith that foretold that the *mahdi* would appear at the *ka'ba* at the turn of the Islamic century as well as other Hadiths that state he will have the same name as the Prophet and exhibit similar physical attributes. The movement taught that after a long period of deviation from true Islam, the *mahdi* had now appeared to put an end to tyrannical kingship and set up God's reign of justice and peace. They were convinced that once their *mahdi* had revealed himself, all Muslims would pay him allegiance, helping him defeat the forces of the corrupt regimes that would be swallowed up by the earth.[163]

In the Shia world, the rise of Khomeini to power in the Islamic Revolution inspired many Iranians to see him either as the promised "Hidden Imam" returning at the world's end or at least as the representative of the Hidden Imam sent to prepare the way for him. 'Ali Shari'ati, the main ideologue of the Iranian revolution, reinterpreted the Shia concept of *intizar* (the waiting for the return of the Hidden Imam) as an active process of accelerating his coming. All roads lead to the inevitable climax when equality and unity are implemented worldwide—this will be utopia, the end of history, the return of the *mahdi*, and the culmination of the dialectical struggle.[164]

It seems that for many impoverished and oppressed Muslims today awaiting a messianic savior figure to restore Islamic pride and glory, Usama bin-Laden is a *mahdi*-like figure who has achieved mythical proportions and is often likened to Saladin, or even to Muhammad himself. His austere and devout lifestyle, zeal for Islam, reported exploits, legendary riches, and international renown have increased his popular appeal to Muslim masses around the world.[165] His charisma, capabilities, technical know-how, and ability to form alliances across a wide front have given him an aura of messiahship. The staggering magnitude of his exploits in terms of victims and destruction and his gift for public relations have made him the darling of Muslim masses. His tirades against the West remind one of the railings of Old Testament prophets against the heathen oppressors of God's people, while his choice of the Twin Towers in New York as a symbol of American arrogance and immoral pagan corruption reminds one of Babylon the Great as the symbol of all human evil and anti-God rebellion in the book of Revelation. These symbolic gestures are not lost on his Muslim audience though they might appear incomprehensible to secular Western reporters. With the destruction of his bases in Afghanistan his popularity may eventually fade, but Muslims all over the world will keep looking for such a *mahdi* figure to save them from their humiliating lot and restore Islam and Muslim society to their former glory.

Radical Islamic fundamentalists thus see themselves as God's sword of wrath in his dealing with human rebellion, immorality, and paganism in the cataclysmic end-time scenario. They are confident of the importance of their role in God's plan and of the ultimate triumph of God's cause no matter how great the sacrifices demanded of them in the meantime.

11

"You Are Not to Say, 'It Is a Conspiracy!'"[166]

CONSPIRACY THEORIES
AND ANTI-SEMITISM

INTRODUCTION

In the Garden of Eden, Adam blamed Eve for causing his sin, while Eve blamed the Serpent for hers. Since then the "blame game" and scapegoating have been favorite human pastimes with groups and individuals from all manner of backgrounds blaming others for their problems. Indiscriminate bloodshed becomes morally easier to practice when external enemies can be held responsible for all misfortunes. These scapegoats are then demonized as evil incarnate—tools of the devil that should be fought against by all and every means.

Islamic fundamentalists have developed many bizarre conspiracy theories over the years. They identify secularism in all its forms, the Christian West, Judaism (especially Zionism), and

Freemasonry as part of a worldwide plot to exterminate true Islam. Governments in most Muslim states encourage these conspiracy theories as a way of deflecting pressure from themselves and turning the anger and frustrations of the masses against external enemies. These external scapegoats are understood to be the source of all the problems besetting society, nation, and the worldwide Muslim community.

CHRISTIAN CONSPIRACY THEORIES

Throughout its long history, Christianity has also been guilty of identifying and persecuting scapegoats. Anti-Semitism and the persecution of heretics were dominant themes during the medieval and early Reformation church eras, and both have left a bitter legacy, with Anti-Semitism culminating in the holocaust.

Many contemporary Christian fundamentalists see liberal secular humanism as the great enemy that, since the Enlightenment, has conspired against Christianity and its values. Atheism, socialism, liberalism, Marxism, and Freemasonry are all seen as products of the evil Enlightenment. Secular humanist and liberal elites are viewed as deliberately infiltrating all power centers in order to impose their godless ideologies on an unsuspecting public. Extremists on the fringes of the religious right in America view all opposing camps as part of an evil Antichrist conspiracy. Taken to the extreme, these assumptions can lead to the belief that opponents are utterly evil and thus must be destroyed.[167] During the cold-war era, godless communism was perceived as the main threat to Western Christian civilization, and groups like the John Birch Society accused secular liberals in the West of being communist agents encouraging socialism and internationalism, with the ultimate goal of creating a one-world socialist government. The United Nations was seen as part of this conspiracy to build a New World Order, and fiendish "Insiders" were posited as the leaders of the conspiracy. These were viewed as Illuminati-Freemasons having an unbroken link back to the French Revolution. Such theories are now coupled to anti-Semitic and anti-Black strands prevalent in Christian Identity, White Supremacist, and neo-Nazi ideologies.[168]

Since the collapse of communism and the end of the cold war, more attention has been directed toward the involvement of the United Nations and United States in international conflicts such as the Gulf War. For many on the extreme Christian right in the United States, the federal government and its agencies are the real enemy, selling out to a United Nations-backed New World Order controlled by foreigners who are bent on weakening America and denying its citizens their God-given and constitutionally-guaranteed rights. The militias, in particular, are organizing themselves and conducting weapons-training exercises so as to be able to fight these conspiratorial enemies in due time.[169]

For some Christian fundamentalists, especially at the extreme end of the pro-Israel dispensationalist spectrum and the Christian-Zionist movement, Islam is the primary enemy of our day, challenging true Christianity for control of the world. Some of their rhetoric suggests a shift of inherent racism, previously directed at Jews and Blacks, in the direction of Muslims.

ISLAMIC FUNDAMENTALIST CONSPIRACY THEORIES

Islamic fundamentalist conspiracy theories are rooted in feelings of frustration, humiliation, and rage cultivated over centuries of weakness, colonialism, dependency, and the loss of Muslim dominance in politics and culture. Jews, Christians, and secularists are the favorite scapegoats in these theories and are usually described as satanic enemies of Islam bent on its destruction.

Traditional Islam saw Jews and Christians living in Muslim lands as protected communities (*dhimmis*) because they were "people of the Book" who had received a valid revelation from God even though it has since been superseded by Islam. Fundamentalists, however, use the historic opposition of Jews and Christians to Muhammad mentioned in the Quran and Hadith to prove uninterrupted Christian and Jewish hatred for Islam since its inception. This hatred has been expressed in continual efforts throughout history to divide, weaken, and destroy Islam. Fundamentalists claim Jews and Christians have rejected the clear message of God through Muhammad and are therefore to be treated as unbelievers (*kuffar*)—a category much more detrimental to its bearers. The Jews and Christians of the seventh century are seen as identical with the Jews and Christians of today, so the "Christian Crusading West" in its contemporary post-colonialist forms, together with the Jews and the Zionists, are viewed as eternal enemies of Islam.

Secularism is also seen as being part of a sinister Western plot to undermine Islam. Secularized Muslims are viewed as anti-Islamic foreign agents.[170] Islamic fundamentalists see an evil trinity of secularism, the Christian West, and Jewish Zionism combining to destroy Islam. Rulers in Muslim states friendly to the West are perceived as puppets of these enemies, betraying their countries into dependence and secularization.

Qutb in Egypt and Khomeini in Iran used their influential writings to instigate hatred toward Jews and Christians. Their followers among Sunni and Shia radicals have imbibed these ideas and developed them in a continuous process of cross-fertilization.

Qutb claimed that there was a worldwide conspiracy of the Crusading Christian West, Marxist Communism, and World Jewry against true Islam. These three forces were *jahiliyya* at its worst, enemies of God always plotting the destruction of Islam. Modern imperialism is a masked Crusade by the Christian West (aided by the Jews) to attain world domination.[171] Hostility to Islam has been inherited, inherent, and latent in the West since Crusader days. Western scholars of Islam (Orientalists) transmitted the distorted versions of Islam absorbed during the Crusades, and secular Europe inherited the contempt for Muslims from religious Europe. These irrational prejudices were encouraged by Western imperialism that saw Islam as the main obstacle in its drive for world dominion. This anti-Islamic spirit unites all Western states and cultures.[172]

Qutb's disciples included the radical Egyptian group *Takfir wal-Hijra* which stressed an international Jewish conspiracy and the need to fight it, accusing the Jews of seducing humanity to idol-worship and of spreading corruption and immorality all over the world. Another Egyptian radical group impacted by Qutb, *al-Jihad*, viewed Christians as the first enemy to be dealt with and was heavily involved in anti-Coptic activities. *Jihad* accused Muslim rulers of obeying Jews and Christians and opening up Muslim countries to exploitation. Its spiritual leader, Sheikh 'Abd al-Rahman, issued a *fatwa* legitimizing the killing and robbing of Christians who were anti-Muslim.[173]

Ayatollah Khomeini of Iran had much to say about the conspiracies of Jews and Christians against Islam:

> Since its inception, Islam was afflicted with the Jews who distorted the reputation of Islam by assaulting and slandering it, and this has continued to our present day. The Crusades made the Christian West realize that Islam with its laws and beliefs was the biggest obstacle to their control and domination of the world. That is why they harbored resentment and treated it

unjustly. Then more than three centuries ago, came the evil colonists who found in the Muslim world their long sought object. To achieve their ambitions they laboured to create the conditions which would lead to the annihilation of Islam. Missionaries, Orientalists, the information media—all are in the service of the colonialist countries and all are guilty of distorting Islam in a way that has caused many Muslims to steer away from it and not find their way back to it. While Islam is the religion of struggle for right, justice, freedom and independence, those enemies have portrayed it in a distorted manner, even in the academic world, aiming at extinguishing its flame and robbing it of its revolutionary character. They teach that Islam has no relevance to society and government and is only concerned with private rituals. These enemies have implanted their falsehoods in the minds of the Muslim people with the help of their agents, and have managed to eliminate Islam's judiciary and political laws from the sphere of application, replacing them by European laws. The colonialists and their lackeys claim there is a separation between state and religion, so they can isolate Islam from the affairs of society and keep the ulama' away from the people. When they have separated and isolated us they can take away our resources and rule us.[174]

Ayatollah Khamenei, Khomeini's successor as Supreme Guardian of the Islamic Republic of Iran, labels the United States and Israel as enemies of Iran and of Islam. America is afraid of Islamic Iran's influence on the Muslims of the world because it has stirred up Muslims everywhere to start fighting and expressing their Islamic feelings. Khamenei posits a struggle during the last twenty years between two competitive camps on the world political scene—the camp of arrogance led by America and the Islamic camp led by the Islamic Republic of Iran. Khamenei reviews the history of United States interference in Iran—a history of "America delivering blows to us, betraying us, stabbing us in the back by plotting coups d'etat. . . ." In the Iraq-Iran war, America supported Iraq against Iran. America has harmed Iran more than anyone else, and it fully deserves the title "The Great Satan" because "it engages in evil, in treachery, in murder and because it is arrogant."[175]

Iranian revolutionary hate-discourse against America affected Sunni fundamentalist groups who realized its effectiveness. For example, the World Islamic Front issued a statement, "Jihad Against Jews and Crusaders," in which the United States was identified as the main enemy of Islam, allied to the Jews, for occupying Islamic holy land in the Arabian Peninsula, and for fighting the Iraqi and Palestinian peoples: "All these crimes and sins committed by the Americans are a clear declaration of war on God, his messenger, and Muslims." The Front issued a *fatwa* declaring it an individual duty (*fard 'ayn*) on all Muslims to kill Americans and their allies wherever possible in order to liberate the Islamic holy places from their grip and to drive out their armies from all Muslim lands.[176]

Usama bin-Laden accuses world Christianity, allied to Zionist Jewry and led by the United States, Britain, and Israel, of attacking the whole Muslim world.[177] This conspiracy is the great enemy, an infidel Crusader-Jewish alliance, which under the cover of the United Nations has massacred Muslims in Palestine, Iraq, Lebanon, Kashmir, Philippines, Somalia, Chechnya, Bosnia, and other places.[178] Bin-Laden also accuses the Western powers of plotting to divide the Arab world into many mini-states. However, the greatest outrage of all is the stationing of infidel American troops in Saudi Arabia, the holy land of Islamic revelation and of the two holy mosques.[179]

As a result of this propaganda, radical Islamic groups have developed a deep loathing for the West. They perceive it as atheistic and materialistic, denying the hereafter, rejecting any accountability to God, and aiming at political, economic, and cultural hegemony in the world. Western societies are depicted as being driven only by greed and the lust for power, encouraging cutthroat capitalist competition and having no pity for the losers. The United States as the Great Satan has become the symbol of the modern, evil, Western-capitalist Crusader-Jewish culture.

Anti-Semitism

As a result of the holocaust, anti-Jewish sentiments now characterize mainly marginal Christian fundamentalist groups, with virulent anti-Semitism being restricted to the extreme fringes. In fact, many of the more mainline groups, especially the dispensationalists, are positively pro-Jewish and pro-Zionist.

Some in the extreme right in America identify the real enemy behind all destructive forces as a small cabal of international bankers, Freemasons, and Illuminati[180] who have planned all the catastrophes of this century, including communism and Nazism, in order to prepare the world for the implementation of their New World Order. These conspiracy theories combine apocalyptic fears and millennial expectations linked to well-documented strands of racist, anti-Semitic, and anti-Freemason themes popular in Christian Identity, White Supremacist, and neo-Nazi ideologies. The secretive, manipulating, and deceitful enemy is seen as linked to demonic, anti-Christian powers. From here it is but a small step to identify most of these conspirators as Jews, reverting to older Western anti-Semitic stereotypes, both religious and racist.

Jews are seen as the seed of Satan, bent on destroying the pure Aryan race and on achieving total world domination.[181]

On the Muslim side, anti-Semitism has become a marker of most fundamentalist movements who, as a result of the Israel-Palestinian conflict, have imbibed much of modern Western-racist anti-Semitism in addition to the traditional anti-Jewish strand of the Quran and Hadith. Anti-Semitism has now infected mainstream Muslim society, especially in the Arab world, as a result of Qutb's invective. Qutb used racist stereotypes and forgeries of Western anti-Semitism such as the "Protocols of the Elders of Zion" (translated into Arabic and widely distributed in the Muslim world).[182] As a result, Islamic fundamentalism today sees itself involved in a cosmic struggle against "the Jews" who are allied to Satan and represent all evil in the world.[183]

For Qutb, modern-day Jews are identical to their forefathers at the time of Muhammad, who opposed Islam from the moment of its revelation.[184] Since then, all Jews have always been wicked enemies of Islam, and the contemporary Muslim community continues to be attacked by the very same Jews and their evil machinations and double-dealings. Anyone who tempts Muslims to leave their religion can only be a Jewish agent.[185]

Qutb accuses the Jews of conspiring to poison the Islamic heritage in order to confuse Muslims and weaken their faith. Jews are inherently evil because all through the ages they have rebelled against God. As a result, they have become creatures who kill, massacre, and defame the prophets, and from whom one can only expect the spilling of human blood and the use of any evil means to further their conspiracies. Jews are characterized by ingratitude, selfishness, fanaticism, and hatred for all others, always fomenting dissension in their host societies, exploiting all disasters to profit from the misery of others. They utilize usury to accumulate wealth, infiltrate societies, and dominate the whole world.[186]

Qutb states that Jews have been behind every misfortune which befell the Muslims through the ages, using conspiracies and treachery to achieve their aims. Zionism is but the latest in the long line of Jewish plots against Islam. He identifies modern secular philosophy and culture as a trap laid by worldwide Judaism in order to destroy barriers of creed, weaken society and government, and enable it to penetrate every country with its "satanic usurious activity" which will finally "deliver the proceeds of all human toil into the hands of the great usurious Jewish financial institutions."[187] He also claims that Orientalism has been infiltrated by Jews who poison Western academic studies of Islam. Jews have even infiltrated Muslim states in the guise of political leaders who lead their people astray: "Therefore the struggle between Islam and the Jews continues in force and will continue, because the Jews will be satisfied only with the destruction of this religion (Islam)."[188]

The Internet displays several Islamic web pages that combine radical Islamic views on politics and power with blatant anti-Semitism of the modern Western racial sort. One example is the "*al-Bayan*" site whose chief editor is Jamaaluddin al-Haidar. When dealing with Jews, it combines references to Quranic and Hadith sources derogatory of Jews with modern Western anti-Jewish discourse such as the "Protocols of the Elders of Zion" and articles obviously gleaned from the Christian neo-Nazi fringe, such as: "The Truth About the Talmud: An Expose on the Roots of Zionism" and "EXPOSED! The AIPAC Tapes Revisited: Evidence of Zionist stranglehold over Clinton White House and US Congress."[189] In an article in which Haidar calls on Muslims of various convictions to drop their petty internal quarrels (the lesser *kufr*) in order to unite in fighting the "greater *kufr*," he names the Jews as the common enemy, stating:

They [the Jews] are vampires, and vampires do not live on vampires. They cannot live only among themselves. They must subsist on Christians and other people not of their race. If you do not exclude them, in less than 200 years our descendants will be working in the fields to furnish them sustenance while they will be in the counting houses rubbing their hands. (i.e. Jewish dominated Wall Street in New York City).[190]

Usama bin-Laden's views reveal a mixture of traditional and modern anti-Jewish sentiments. In the past, Jews attacked the Prophets as well as Jesus and Mary. They have always engaged in killing, raping and stealing.[191] The Jews want to divide the Muslim world, enslave it, and loot its wealth, and they use Western powers to achieve these aims,[192] even installing governments in America that serve as their agents and do their bidding.[193]

Many observers are troubled by this new aspect of Islamic anti-Semitism which is now pouring out its hate propaganda through all available outlets in the Muslim world, including mainstream and governmental media. This new type of anti-Semitism is linked to modern European irrational ideologies such as Fascism and Nazism. Traditional Muslims did not see the Jews who had resisted Muhammad as archetypes of Jews in all times and places. These observers stress the overall record of Islamic civilization's tolerance of Jews over many centuries, especially as compared to that of European Christianity, seeing them as *dhimmis* and as a legitimate community of the 'people of the book' (*ahl al-kitab*). In contrast, modern Islamic fundamentalist anti-Semitism, reacting to the creation of the state of Israel, sees Jews everywhere and at all times as involved in a sinister plot to destroy Islam. Selectively using the same Quran and Hadith sources as the traditionalists, it blurs the distinctions between anti-Semitism, anti-Zionism, and anti-Judaism, arriving at the view that all Jews are the enemies of God and the perennial arch-conspirators against Islam. Islamists have been infected by modern extremist anti-Semitism recycled as the authentic ideological view of Islam, conveniently targeting all Jews as scapegoats in order to excuse modern Muslim weakness. Fundamentalist Islam has linked modern Western anti-Semitism to negative source texts and to the modern political context of the state of Israel, developing a virulent, extreme, and dangerous new form of anti-Semitism. Everything is now viewed through this ideological anti-Jewish prism.[194]

ANTI-SEMITIC ALLIANCE?

It is evident that extreme radicals, both Christian and Islamic, find common ground on the anti-Semitic theme and are evolving an alliance of sorts. For example, Ahmed Rami, a former lieutenant in the Moroccan army who fled to Sweden following his involvement with military coups in Morocco in the early 1970s, has set up a radio station called Radio Islam that broadcasts and publishes virulent anti-Semitic material. His efforts target Zionism and the Jews as the "only one enemy" of Islam and of mankind and include excerpts from the "Protocols of the Elders of Zion" and American right wing racist, supremacist, and anti-Semitic materials. He has forged links with both American and Russian anti-Semitic groups, sees Jewish conspiracies behind all Western and some Arab regimes (which he terms "Judaeocracies"), and claims that a "Zionist Mafia" and Jewish intellectual terrorism have overpowered Western systems (as in Sweden). From his perspective, "the power over banks, mass media and commercial and industrial life is in the hands of a small group of 'the chosen people.' All education in schools and universities is carried on in a way which is favorable to the 'master race.'"[195] Ahmad also publishes a letter from a listener that urges "it is time for Muslims and Christians to stop fighting each other and see the REAL enemy! [i.e., the Jews]"[196]

12

Right Attitudes

AN EVANGELICAL RESPONSE TO ISLAMIC FUNDAMENTALISM

INTRODUCTION

This book has explored Islamic fundamentalism as a phenomenon of human religious behavior by using comparisons with the history of Christianity and with evangelicalism to help us better understand the movement. As humans created in God's image, we all have that vacuum within that only God can fill, feel the need for spiritual meaning in our lives, and express our religious feelings in a variety of similar ways across cultural and religious barriers.

The similarities noted in human responses and behaviors do not, however, address the objective truth content of the different religions. As an evangelical Christian I firmly believe that God has revealed himself and his will for us fully and uniquely only in the Bible and through Jesus Christ (God manifest in the flesh) and that faith in Christ is the only way to salvation—it is by God's grace that men can be saved through faith and not by works or human merit. True Christianity must be centered on Christ, the cross, and the Bible. On a human level, institutional Christianity has made many sad and terrible mistakes throughout its history, but at its very core it is the unique person of Christ and the uniqueness of the cross of Christ that differentiates the true biblical faith from all other religions. Other religions possess some truths that God graciously embeds in different human contexts to point men to himself—"all truth is God's truth" wherever it is found—and there are many redemptive analogies and hidden keys to the gospel in all religions and cultures, as God has not left himself without a witness. But outside of faith in Christ as revealed in the Bible, other religions offer only a human way of attempting to work out their own salvation by their own efforts and merits. I do not view Muhammad as a true prophet or the Quran as a divine revelation.

A CHRISTIAN RESPONSE

As followers of Christ, there are several responses available to us. The first has to do with "being wise as serpents but harmless as doves," meaning we are not to be naïve in assessing Islam nor fall for the politically correct representations of Islam offered by politicians, the media, and liberal church leaders. Terrorists are not simply a handful of extremists who are not real Muslims. Rather, they spring out of a variegated Muslim religious structure that has always offered the possibility of interpreting some of its sources as justifications for violence. Historically, many Muslim reform movements have engaged in Holy War, using a return to the origins as their legitimization. Literal interpretations of the Quran and

Hadith certainly support the more aggressive stance, especially when the doctrine of abrogation is accepted.[197] It would be naïve to ignore the conviction that Islam—not just Islamic fundamentalism—is centrally about power and that Muslims have succeeded in gaining a beachhead in the West for their bid to power as God's chosen people. Muslims are guaranteed God's promise of success in the political venture of subduing all of humanity to God's religion of Islam. It is only the quietist, pacifist, modernist, and liberal Muslims who have to spiritualize the message and reinterpret it to suit their more peaceful stances. This they often do while facing violent assaults on their liberty and life in Muslim societies where traditionalists and fundamentalists set very strict limits to the permissible expression of opinions. Even in the West they are often subjected to severe social pressure or ostracism, and in extreme cases (Salman Rushdie, for example) to death threats supported by religious edicts.

Some evangelicals are entering into dialogue with "moderate"[198] Muslims in order to encourage a reform of Islam and a reformulation of its basic doctrines in pluralistic and peaceful terms. It is difficult to predict whether this has any chance of success or if it just plays into the hands of a wider Muslim agenda to infiltrate Christian centers to their advantage. It is certainly important to know and acknowledge the differences between fundamentalists and the various other forms of Islam whatever their labels, but it is also important to realize that Muslims seeking dialogue often have their own rather different agenda and often try to impose limiting conditions on their Christian counterparts without accepting any such limits themselves. They cleverly exploit both their own victim aura and the guilt complexes of Western Christians burdened with the legacy of racism, colonialism, and imperialism.

Another appropriate response is to realize that all humans, both Christian and Muslim, are fallen beings born in sin and needing

God's saving intervention on their behalf through faith in Jesus Christ and his substitutionary death on the cross. In this sense there is no difference between us (see the first six chapters of Romans). All are under the bondage of sin, which is the prevailing human condition. Sin besets all of us, although its cultural expressions may differ. Christians and Muslims all need to come to the foot of the cross as beggars seeking God's forgiveness and mercy. While clearly seeing the evils in Islam, we must be always ready to repent of our own sins and shortcomings. Those of us who have experienced God's forgiveness and salvation have the duty of sharing it with those who have not—we are witnesses to our Muslim friends of what God has done for us in Christ, and the only attitude possible in light of the many failures and sins of Christian history (as well as our own) is one of love, humility, and service. We must follow in the steps of our Lord who came to serve and to save. There is no room for arrogance or self-righteousness, only for the attitude of "there but for the grace of God go I." We must persevere in pointing to and reflecting Christ as the only way to salvation for all sinners who believe, noting the similarities of our human condition before God.

We need to respect the zeal Muslim fundamentalists have for their religion and its propagation, their devotion to God as they understand him, and their diligence in pursuing his perceived will on earth. At the same time, we must realize it is "without knowledge," based on wrong premises, and resulting in evil outcomes. I also believe God allows movements such as this to prosper for a time in order to provoke us Christians to jealousy and to push us to be sincere, zealous, and surrendered to the cause of Christ and the gospel.

Having said all that, we must surely reject the "end justifies the means" approach of fundamentalist extremists and condemn it as utterly evil, leading inexorably to the terrorist atrocities of recent times. We must also demand that "moderate" Muslims unconditionally condemn such acts and distance themselves from the perpetrators without indulging in the common tendency to limit all such condemnations by finding excuses and justifications for the rage and hate that motivate terrorists' deeds.

Recognizing the positive aspects of the wider Islamic civilization, art, and culture we also recognize its failure as a human institution to provide ultimate answers to the plight of humanity. Islamic fundamentalism, like other utopian political ideologies offering total solutions to all problems of humanity, leads inexorably to violence and tyranny. As evangelical Christians, we realize that contemporary enemies of the gospel include Western secularism, modernism, liberal humanism, and liberal Christianity, all of which deny the very existence of God, His salvation in Christ, and the validity of His moral principles. These movements attack true Christianity at every opportunity and marginalize it in the public square—in education, politics, the media, and law. On a human level, we are thus closer to theistic religions like Islam than to the opinion-forming elites of our own societies. This opens the door to limited co-operation with certain Muslims on specific issues that reflect shared norms for the common good of our societies, while clearly delineating our belief differences and the limits of our co-operation. We must always be careful of the "One Way Street" approach of Muslims who often lay preconditions on co-operation with Christians, such as the prohibition of evangelization among Muslims. We cannot compromise our right to bear witness to Christ as savior and to the missionary duty of the Church, just as Muslims would never deny their duty to propagate the call of Islam.

Finally, we must trust that God is in control,[199] shaking Muslim societies in order to bring about a turning of hearts from among them to Christ. While nations and societies are being polarized by recent events, Muslims around the world are increasingly disenchanted with Islam and are turning to Christ. God is ever controlling the rise and fall of nations and leaders to further the cause of the gospel, while judging both his own people and the unbelieving forces that persecute them.

THE COLD WAR PARADIGM

During the long years of communist rule in the former Soviet Union, there was no doubt that the Soviet regime was evil, bent on world domination, denying its own citizens basic human rights, suppressing religion, and instigating countless rebellions and guerilla wars around the world. That, however, did not lead Christians to conclude that all Russians were evil or that there was no need to get the gospel into the Soviet Union and to help the underground church.

In a similar vein, it is clear that Islam as a political system, especially in its fundamentalist form, is an evil totalitarian system that is rabidly anti-Christian and instigating terror around the world. This should not lead us to conclude that all Muslims are evil or that we should avoid any contact with them. On the contrary, it should lead us to see them as individuals for whom Christ died and to pursue them all the more with Christ's love, compassion, and offer of the gospel. It should also lead us to be more knowledgeable about conditions in Muslim countries and to be involved in supporting both missionary outreach and the Christian minorities there who are under severe pressure and in some cases are suffering outright persecution.

CONCLUSION

As I worked on this manuscript, news reached me almost every week of terrorist atrocities around the world in which hundreds of people, mostly Jews and Westerners, were killed. The international network of Islamic fundamentalist terrorism is certainly doing its best to create self-fulfilling conditions for its cataclysmic vision of the end-time struggle against the powers of evil as symbolized by the "Crusading Christian West." Such indiscriminate massacres result in a polarization of positions and in calls for reprisals that could degenerate into the "clash of civilizations" predicted by some observers. May we as Christian believers learn to follow the example of Christ in his attitude of compassion and love—even for the enemies of his people—and in his willingness to suffer even unto the cross.

Glossary

'abd—slave, servant; used in Arabic names combined with one of the names of God

ahl al-kitab—people of the book; Christians and Jews

'alim (*pl.* 'ulama)'—religious scholar, well versed in the Islamic sciences and accepted as an authority in religious matters, especially interpretation of Sharia

'Ali—son-in-law of Muhammad and fourth Caliph; considered by the Shia (along with his descendants) to be the only legitimate ruler of the Muslim world

Allah—the Arabic word for God, related to the biblical Hebrew El, Eloha, Elohim

amir—commander, leader, prince

ayatollah—sign of God; in Shia Islam an honorary title for the highest ranking religious scholar-jurists al-Azhar—the oldest and most authoritative university of Islamic studies in Cairo, Egypt

al-Banna, Hasan—founder of the Muslim Brotherhood in Egypt

al-dajjal—the Antichrist

bid'a—innovation or heresy

dar al-harb—the abode of war, where non-Muslims predominate

dar al-Islam—the abode of peace under Muslim political dominion

da'wa—the call or invitation for humans to accept Islam; Muslim missionary activity

dhimmis—non-Muslims of a recognized monotheistic religion living as protected minorities in the Islamic state

faqih—legal experts trained in the sources of religion; interpreters of Sharia

fard—a religious command or duty according to Sharia

fatwa—a legal opinion given by a scholar-jurist authorized to do so (a mufti)

fiqh—Islamic jurisprudence, the science of applying Sharia

fitna—sedition, discord, strife; the breakdown of law and order which is evil and must be subdued

fitra—the original nature of humans; their innate disposition as created by God in harmony with the ultimate religion of Islam

Hadith—the collected traditions containing narratives of Muhammad's sayings and deeds outside the Quran

haj—the pilgrimage to Mecca, one of the five pillars of Islam

hijra—the emigration (flight) of Muhammad and his Companions from Mecca to Medina in 622 AD which marks the beginning of the Muslim calendar

hakimiyya—God's sovereign rule over all

ijma'—scholarly consensus on a matter of Sharia interpretation

ijtihad—legal process of independent individual reasoning in interpreting Muslim Scriptures and law when no specific texts on the subject are available imam—literally, "he who stands before;" a prayer leader and teacher in a mosque or authority in religious sciences; in Shia Islam, the venerated descendants of Muhammad through 'Ali and Fatimah, the only legitimate rulers of the world Muslim community

islah—reform

Islam—submission and surrender to God, recognizing God's unity and Muhammad's apostleship

istishhad—martyrdom; losing one's life as an act of witness in God's cause

jahiliyya—the state of pagan ignorance and barbarity in pre-Islamic Arabian society

jama'a—a community, group, society, especially a religious community

jihad—literally, "effort or struggle," usually meaning Holy War in God's cause

jizya—poll tax collected from protected (dhimmi) non-Muslims in a Muslim state

ka'ba—the central and sacred cube-shaped shrine in the great mosque at Mecca, the center of Muslim pilgrimage and the direction in which Muslims face in prayer

kafir (*pl.* kuffar)—infidel, unbeliever; one who rejects, denies, and repudiates the revelation given by God through Muhammad, and as such worthy of the death sentence

khalifa—steward, deputy and successor to Muhammad; Caliph; later understood as God's vice-regent on earth; title of the Muslim rulers of the Islamic state following Muhammad

madhab—one of the four main schools of jurisprudence in Islam

madrasa—religious school

mahdi—the "rightly guided one;" the eschatological messianic savior and purifier of religion who will save humanity from oppression and establish a reign of justice and peace

mufti—jurisprudent who issues fatwas

mujahid—a person dedicated to fighting in a jihad

mujtahid—a Shia scholar-jurist with authority to give an independent opinion on matters of Sharia

qiyas—legal reasoning by analogy as a source of Sharia

Quran—the Arabic book containing the revelation to Muhammad; the primary "Holy Book" of Islam, accepted as God's word, eternal, perfectly preserved, and infallible

Al-Rashidun—the "rightly guided" Caliphs; the first four Muslim rulers following Muhammad's death

Salafiyya—a movement of revival and reform calling for a return to the example of the pious forebears, (the salaf)

shahada—the obligatory declaration of faith "there is no god but Allah and Muhammad is his messenger"

shahid (*pl.* shuhada)'—martyr; literally, "witness;" one who loses his life in God's cause

Sharia—the sacred law of Islam; literally, "the path;" its sources are the Quran, Sunna, analogical reasoning, and scholarly consensus

Shia—the branch of Islam that supports the claims of Muhammad's son-in-law, 'Ali, and his descendants to the leadership of Islam

shirk—polytheism, idolatry the association of partners with God. A major sin in Islam.

shura—consultation; mentioned in the Quran in reference to Muslim rulers consulting with others on the affairs of state; used as the basis for concepts of democracy in Islam

Sira—the official biographies of the life of Muhammad considered as part of Sunna alongside Hadith

Sufism—the mystical movement of Islam that permeates all branches and sects

Sunna—the "Way" of the Prophet accepted as the supreme model for emulation; his lifestyle, mannerisms, sayings, and deeds as narrated in the Hadith traditions and the biographies (sira) of Muhammad; considered part of the divine revelation second only to the Quran in authority, and legally binding

Sunnis—followers of the main "orthodox" branch of Islam; the majority (85%) of Muslims

tafsir—interpretation, commentary, usually on the Quran

tajdid—renewal

takfir—the legal declaration of an individual, community, or institution as infidel or apostate and worthy of the death sentence

taqlid—blind imitation in legal interpretation, often of the leaders of the legal schools in Islam or of famous later commentators and jurists

tawhid—unity, oneness; the affirmation of God's absolute divine unity, the basis of monotheistic Islam

umma—the community or nation of Islam composed of all Muslims worldwide

zakat—obligatory religious tax which is one of the five pillars of Islam

zulm—the Quranic term for wrong-doing, perversion, oppression, and tyranny

BIBLIOGRAPHY

BOOKS

Abanes, Richard, 1996. *American Militias: Rebellion, Racism and Religion,* Downers Grove, IL: Intervarsity Press.

Abdelnasser, W. M., 1994. *The Islamic Movement in Egypt,* London: Kegan Paul International.

al-Banna, Hasan, 1978. *Five Tracts of Hasan al-Banna (1906–1949): A Selection from the Majmu'at Rasa'il al-Imam al-Shahid,* Berkeley: University of California Press.

al-Yassini, Ayman, 1985. *Religion and State in the Kingdom of Saudi Arabia,* Boulder, CO: Westview Press.

Antoun, Richard T., and Mary E. Hegland, eds., 1987. *Religious Resurgence: Contemporary Cases in Islam, Christianity and Islam,* Syracuse, NY: Syracuse University Press.

'Azzam, 'Abdullah, ed., n.d. *Defense of the Muslim Lands,* London: Ahle Sunnah Wal Jama'at.

————, 1996. *Join the Caravan*, London: Azzam Publications.

Burrel, Robert M. ed., 1989. *Islamic Fundamentalism*, London: Royal Asiatic Society.

Choueiri, Youssef, M., 1990. *Islamic Fundamentalism*, London: Cassel Printer Publishers.

Dekmejian, Hrair, 1985. *Islam In Revolution: Fundamentalism in the Arab World*, Syracuse, NY: Syracuse University Press.

Donohue, John J. and John L. Esposito, eds., 1982. *Islam in Transition: Muslim Perspectives*, New York and Oxford: Oxford University Press.

Ende and Steinbach, eds., 1984. *Der Islam in der Gegenwart*, Munich: C.H. Beck.

Esposito, John, 1988. *Islam: The Straight Path*, New York: Oxford University Press.

————, 1992. *The Islamic Threat: Myth Or Reality?*, New York: Oxford University Press.

Faraj, Muhammad Abdelsalam, *The Neglected Duty (al-farida al-gha'iba)*, in J. J. G. Jansen, 1986. *The Neglected Duty: The Creed of Sadat's Assassins and Islamic Resurgence in the Middle East*, New York: Macmillan.

Hefner, Robert W., ed.,1993. *Conversion to Christianity*, Berkeley: University of California Press.

Hopwood, Derek. 1991. *Egypt: Politics and Society 1945-1990*, London: Harper Collins Academic.

Ibrahim, Abdul-Maajid, and Darbaalah, 1997. *In Pursuit of Allah's Pleasure*, London: Azzam Publications.

Jabbour, Nabeel T., 1993. *The Rumbling Volcano: Islamic Fundamentalism In Egypt*, Pasadena, CA: William Carey Library.

Kepel, Gilles, 1985. *The Prophet and The Pharaoh: Muslim Extremism in Egypt*, London: al-Saqi.

Macdonald, Andrew, 1996. *The Turner Diaries*, New York:

Barricade Books.

Maddy-Weitzman and Inbar, eds., 1997. *Islamic Radicalism in the Greater Middle East*, London: Frank Cass.

Maley, William, ed., 1998. *Fundamentalism Reborn? Afghanistan and the Taliban,* London: Hurst and Company.

Marty, Martin and R. Scott Appleby, eds., 1991. *Fundamentalisms Observed,* Chicago: Chicago University Press.

————, 1993. *Fundamentalisms and the State,* Chicago: University of Chicago Press.

Mawdudi, Abul A'la, 1982. *Let Us be Muslims,* edited by K. Murad, Leicester: The Islamic Foundation.

————, 1984. *The Islamic Movement: Dynamics of Values, Power and Change*, North Haledon, New Jersey: Islamic Publications International.

————, 1986. *The Islamic Way of Life,* Leicester: The Islamic Foundation.

————, 1997. *Jihad fi Sabilillah (Jihad in Islam)*, Birmingham: UK Islamic Dawah Centre.

————, 1997. *Towards Understanding Islam,* Leicester: The Islamic Foundation.

Murad, Khurram, 1996. *Key to al-Baqarah: The Longest Surah of the Qur'an,* Leicester: The Islamic Foundation.

Musk, Bill, 1992. *Passionate Believers,* Tunbridge Wells: MARC Europe/Monarch Publications.

Nadwi, Abul Hasan Ali, 1983. *Muslims in the West: The Message and Mission,* edited by K. Murad, Leicester: The Islamic Foundation.

Nettler, Ronald L., 1987. *Past Trials and Present Tribulations: A Muslim Fundamentalist's View of the Jews,* Oxford: Pergamon Press.

Pearse, Meic, 1998. *The Great Restoration: The Religious*

Radicals of the 16th and 17th Centuries, Carlisle: Paternoster Press.

Qutb, Sayyid, 1979. *In the Shade of the Qur'an,* Vol. 30, London: MWH Publishers.

————, 1990. *Milestones,* Indianapolis: American Trust.

Reeves, Simon, 2000. *The New Jackals: Ramzi Yousef, Osama bin Laden and the Future of Terrorism,* London: Andre Deutsch.

Roy, Olivier, 1994. *The Failure of Political Islam,* London: I.B. Tauris.

Rubin, Barry and Judith Colp Rubin, eds., 2002. *Anti-American Terrorism and the Middle East: A Documentary Reader,* New York: Oxford University Press.

Shariati, Ali, 1979. *On The Sociology of Islam,* trans. Hamid Algar, Berkeley: Mizan Press.

————, 1981a. *Man and Islam,* trans. Marjani, Houston: Free Islamic Literature.

————, 1981b. *Martyrdom: Arise and Bear Witness,* trans. Ghassemi, Tehran: Ministry of Islamic Guidance.

————, 1986. *What Is to Be Done: The Enlightened Thinkers and an Islamic Renaissance,* Houston: IRIS.

Westerlund, David, ed., 1996. *Questioning the Secular State,* London: Hurst and Company.

Zakariya, Rafiq, 1989. *The Struggle Within Islam: The Conflict Between Religion and Politics,* New York: Penguin Books.

CHAPTERS IN BOOKS

Ahmad, Khurshid, 1976. "Islam: Basic Principles and Characteristics," in Khurshid Ahmad, ed., *Islam: Its Meaning and Message,* Leicester: The Islamic Foundation.

Ben-Dor, Gabriel, 1997. "The Uniqueness of Islamic Fundamentalism," in Maddy-Weitzman and Inbar, eds., *Islamic*

Radicalism in the Greater Middle East, London: Frank Cass.

Khomeini, Ruhollah, 1982. "Islamic Government," in Donohue and Esposito, eds. *Islam in Transition: Muslim Perspectives.*

———, ed., 1991. "Interpretation of Surah Al-Hamd," in T. Mutahhari and R. Khumayni, eds., *Light Within Me,* Qum: Ansariyan Publications.

Kostiner, Joseph, 1997. "State, Islam and Opposition in Saudi Arabia," in Maddy-Wizman and Inbar, eds., *Religious Radicalism in the Greater Middle East,* London: Frank Cass.

Lambton, Ann K. S., 1989. "The Clash of Civilizations: Authority, Legitimacy and Perfectibility," in Robert M. Burrel, ed., *Islamic Fundamentalism,* London: Royal Asiatic Society.

Qutb, Sayyid, 1996. "Social Justice in Islam," in W. Shepard, ed., *Sayyid Qutb and Islamic Activism: A Translation and Critical Analysis of "Social Justice in Islam,"* Leiden: E.J. Brill.

Rapoport, David C., 1993. "Comparing Militant Fundamentalist Groups," in Marty and Appleby, eds., *Fundamentalisms and the State,* Chicago: University of Chicago Press.

Saiedi, Nader, 1986. "What is Fundamentalism?" in Hadden and Shupe, eds., *Prophetic Religious and Politics*, New York: Paragon House.

Shariati, Ali, 1982. "Intizar: The Religion of Protest and the Return to Self," in Donohue and Esposito, eds., *Islam in Transition: Muslim Perspectives,* New York: Oxford University Press.

ARTICLES

Abshire, Brian M. "Counter-Cultural Christianity: Militias!" *The Chalcedon Report,* No. 407, June 1999, <http://www.chalcedon.edu/report/99jun/index.htm>.

Abu Ruqaiyah. "The Islamic Legitimacy of the 'Martyrdom Operations'," *Nida'ul Islam,* December/January 1996–7,

<http://www.islam.org.au/articles/16/martyrdom.htm>.

Ahmad, Israr. "The Obligations Muslims Owe to the Qur'an," *Tanzeem-e-Islami*, <http://www.tanzeemorg/warehouse/researchpapers/obligations.html>.

"Ahmad Rami's Idealism," *Pravda* interview with Ahmad Rami, *Radio Islam*, July 15, 1997, <http://www.radioislam/english/toread/pravda.htm>.

al-Haidar, Jamaaluddin. "Sufi-vs-Salafi: The Pot Calls the Kettle Black," <http://www.ummah.net.pk/albayan/editorsdeskSet1.html>.

Al-Mas'ari, Muhammad, "Ruling by Kufr is Haram," *MSANEWS*, December 18, 1997.

Ansari, Hamid. "The Islamic Militants in Egyptian Politics," *International Journal of Middle Eastern Studies*, Vol. 16, 1984. pp. 136–137.

Article 6, *Ain-al-Yaqeen*, September 21, 2001, <http://www.ain-al-aqeen.com/issues/2001921/feat6en.htm>.

bin-Laden, Usama. 1996. "Declaration of War Against the Americans Occupying the Land of the Two Holy Places," <http://www.azzzam.com/html/body_declaration.html>.

Broderick, Greg R.. "The Lunatic Fringes," *The Radical Religious Right Pages*, <http://mother.qrd.org/qrd/www/RRR/lunatic.html>.

Buttner, Friedemann. "The Fundamentalist Impulse and the Challenge of Modernity," *Law and State*, Vol. 55, 1997.

"Conversation with Terror," Interview with Usama bin-Laden in *TIME*, January 11, 1999, pp. 34–35.

Chief Mufti of the Palestinian Police, Sheikh Abd al-Salam Abu Shukheydem, <http://www.memri.org/ia/lA7401.html>.

Dawoud, Khaled, "America's Most Wanted," *Al-Ahram Weekly Online*, Issue No. 552, September 20–26.

"Declaration of The Conference of Islamic Revivalist Movements,"

Friday, November 20, 1998, *MSANEWS*, 24, 11, 1998, <http://msanews.mynet.net/MSANEWS/199811/19981124.24.html>.

Eickelman, Dale F. "Inside the Islamic Reformation," *Wilson Quarterly*, Vol. 22, No 1, Winter 1998, pp. 80–89.

Engel, Richard. "Inside Al-Qaeda: A Window into the World of Militant Islam and the Afghani Alumni," Jane's International Security News, September 28, 2001, <http://www.janes.com/security/inter...ity/news/misc/janes010928_1_n.shtml>.

Feldner, Yotam. "Debating the Religious, Political and Moral Legitimacy of Suicide Bombings," *The Middle East Media and Research Institute Inquiry and Analysis*, No. 53, (May 2, 2001), <http://www.memri.org/ia/lA5301.html>.

Harb, Nabila. "The Truth about Martyrdom in Arab and Islamic Culture." <http://www.freearabvoice.org/issueHumanBombs.htm#text2>.

Jama'at creed, *Azzam Publications*, <http://www.webstorage.com/~azzam/html>

"John Birch Society," *The Public Eye*, Political Research Associates, <http://www.publiceye.org/tooclose/jbs.html>.

Khamenei, Ali. "No Need for Iran-US Negotiations," excerpts from a *khutbah* addressed to Tehran's Friday worshippers on January 16, 1998. MSANEWS, January 27, 1998.

Kramer, Martin. "The Salience of Islamic Anti-Semitism," October 1995, *MSANEWS*, May 19, 1996, <http://msanews.mynet.net/MSANEWS/199605/19960519.1.html>.

Larson, Warren, "How Islam Sees Itself," *Evangelical Missions Quarterly*, Vol. 38, No. 4, October, 2002, pp. 434–441.

Lewis, Bernard. "The Roots of Muslim Rage," *The Atlantic Monthly*, Vol. 266, No. 3, September 1990, pp. 47–60.

Mneimneh, Hassan and Kanan Makiya, "Manual for a Raid," *The New York Review of Books*, January 17, 2002

Nettler, R. "A Modern Confession of Faith and Conception of Religion: Sayyid Qutb's Introduction to the Tafsir, Fi Zilal Al-Qur'an," *British Journal of Middle Eastern Studies*, Vol. 21, No. 1, 1994, pp. 102–114.

Pipes, Daniel. "Muslims Love Bin Laden," New York Post, October 22, 2001

Qa'idat al-jihad, April 24, 2002, quoted by Reuven Paz, "Qa'idat al-Jihad: A New Name on the Road to Palestine," <http://www.ict.org.il/articles/aertcleedet.cfm?articleid=43>.

"Right On!" by Jessie, *Radio Islam,* <http://www.radioislam.net/letters/chrtmus.htm>.

Rashwan, Diaa. "Islamists Crash the Party," Al-Ahram Weekly, Issue No. 447, September 16–22.

———. "A War Over Resources," Al-Ahram Weekly Online, September 20-26, 2001.

Sardar, Ziauddin. "Clinton Provokes a Jihad: Bin Laden vs Hasan-e Sabah," *New Statesman,* August 28, 1998.

Shay, Shaul and Yoram Schweitzer, "The 'Afghan Alumni' Terrorism: Islamic Militants Against the Rest of the World," The International Policy Institute for Counter Terrorism, November 6, 2000, <http://www.ict.org.il/articledet.cfm?articleid=140>.

Shepard, William. "'Fundamentalism' Christian and Islamic," *Religion,* Vol. 17, 1987, pp. 335–378.

Strawson, John. "Encountering Islamic Law," Essay presented at the Critical Legal Conference, New College, Oxford, September 9–12, 1993. "The World Wide Web Virtual Library: Islamic and Middle Eastern Law," <http://www.uel.ac.uk/faculties/socsci/law/jsrps.html>.

"Talking with Terror's Banker," an ABC News interview with Usama bin-Laden conducted by John Miller, May 28, 1998. <http://abcnews.go.com/sections/world/dailynews/terror_980609.html>.

"Terror Suspect," an ABC News interview with Usama bin-Laden conducted by Rahimullah Yousafsai in December 1998, <http://printerfriend...mGLUE=true&GLUEService=ABCNewsArc>.

The Economist, August 6–12th, 1994, "The Fundamentalist Fear," pp. 13–14;

————, August 6–12th, 1994, "A Survey of Islam," pp. 3–18

"Usamah bin-Laden, the Destruction of the Base," an Interview with Usama bin-Laden conducted by Jamal Isma'il and aired June 10, 1999. Published by The Terrorism Research Centre, <http://www.terrorism.com/terrorism/BinLadinTranscript.shtm>.

Weisman, Itzchak, 1997, "Sa'id Hawwa and Islamic Revivalism in Ba'thist Syria," in *Studia Islamica*, Vol. 4, No. 1, February 1997. pp. 131–154.

World Islamic Front Statement, "Jihad Against Jews and Crusaders," <http://www.fas.org/irp/world/para/docs/980223-fatwa.htm>.

Zebiri, Kate. "Muslim Anti-Secularist Discourse in the Context of Muslim-Christian Relations," *Islam and Christian-Muslim Relations,* Vol. 9, No. 1, 1998.

Zeidan, David, "Radical Islam in Egypt: A Comparison of Two Groups," *Middle East Review of International Affairs,* Vol. 3, No. 3, September 1999.

ENDNOTES

INTRODUCTION

[1]Marty and Appleby, *Fundamentalisms Observed,* 814–842.

[2]Sunna is the more general term meaning Muhammad's way— the way he acted, the words he spoke, all seen as a model to be followed by the faithful of all times. The Hadith are the actual narratives containing Muhammad's words and deeds as remembered by his closest companions and collected by various specialists in the first centuries of Islam.

[3]Lewis, "The Roots of Muslim Rage," 47–60.

CHAPTER 1

[4]Eickelman, "Inside the Islamic Reformation," 80–89.

[5]Pearse, *The Great Restoration.*

[6]Quoted in "It Is Now The Year 1415," *The Economist,* August 4, 1994.

[7]Shariati, *On The Sociology Of Islam,* 58; Shariati, *What Is To Be Done*, 8; Shariati, *Man and Islam*, 103, 104.

[8]Shariati, *Man and Islam,* 105.

[9]Shariati, *What Is To Be Done*, 24–25.

[10]Buttner, "The Fundamentalist Impulse and the Challenge of Modernity," 72–73.

[11]Shepard, "'Fundamentalism' Christian and Islamic," 360.

[12]Ibid., 366–367.

[13]Ibid., 360–362.

[14]*The Economist*, August 6-12th, 1994, "The Fundamentalist Fear," 13–14; and *The Economist*, August 6–12th, 1994, "A Survey of Islam," 3–18. In many countries these frustrations first led to Marxist and Maoist movements, e.g. "The Shining Path" of Peru, and the strong Tudeh communist party of Iran.

[15]Hegland, *Religious Resurgence,* 248–249; The dominant elites can be the Westernized secularized elites ruling most Arab countries, or the liberal secular-humanist elites who until recently dominated Western societies and especially the media and academia.

[16]Shepard, "'Fundamentalism' Christian and Islamic," 366.

[17]Westerlund, *Questioning the Secular State,* 1, 6, 8.

[18]Shepard, "'Fundamentalism' Christian and Islamic," 359.

[19]Saiedi, *Prophetic Religions and Politics,* 173–195.

[20]Shepard, "'Fundamentalism' Christian and Islamic," 361.

[21]Robert W. Hefner, *Conversion to Christianity,* 4.

[22]Ibid., 3–4; Large scale conversion to fundamentalist Christianity is especially visible in Latin America and Korea. For Islamic fundamentalism the West seems especially fruitful—in Africa and Asia it is still the *Sufi* forms that seems more attractive to non-Muslims. The great success of fundamentalist Islam lies, of course, in attracting many professing Muslims to its ranks.

[23]Shepard, "'Fundamentalism' Christian and Islamic," 361.

[24]Westerlund, *Questioning the Secular State*, 4–5. In

Christianity, not only fundamentalists, but also most evangelicals subscribe to the inerrancy doctrine.

[25]Shepard, "'Fundamentalism' Christian and Islamic," 366–367; See also Zebiri, *Islam and Christian-Muslim Relations,* 1.

[26]Westerlund, *Questioning the Secular State*, 4–5. See also Shepard, "'Fundamentalism' Christian and Islamic," 360: In Latin America, Liberation Theology adopted a similar revolutionary idiom.

[27]This is, on the whole, true also of Christian fundamentalists in Third World countries.

[28]Shepard, "'Fundamentalism' Christian and Islamic," 360.

[29]Ben-Dor, *Islamic Radicalism in the Greater Middle East,* 242–243.

[30]Luke 20:25.

[31]Ben-Dor, *Islamic Radicalism in the Greater Middle East,* 245.

[32]Roy, *The Failure of Politcal Islam,* 65–67; see also: Ben-Dor, *Islamic Radicalism in the Greater Middle East,* 246–247; Shia martyrdom has a long pedigree beginning with that of 'Ali and Hussein, which are annually commemoratcd in the 'Ashura. Martyrdom as a political and military tool has been especially cultivated by Shia groups in Iran (*Fedayin-i-Islam*) and Lebanon (*Hizbullah*), and the Palestinian Hamas and Islamic Jihad groups, though it appears also in other arenas of Islamic struggle against perceived enemies as in Afghanistan, Chechnya, etc.

CHAPTER 2

[33]Esposito, *Islam: The Straight Path,* 116–118; Dekmejian, *Islam In Revolution,* 12.

[34]Weisman, "Sa'id Hawwa and Islamic Revivalism in Ba'thist

Syria," 132; Choueiri, *Islamic Fundamentalism,* 181.

[35]Ben-Dor, *Islamic Radicalism in the Greater Middle East,* 241.

[36]Dekmejian, *Islam in Revolution,* 9.

[37]Roy, *The Failure of Political Islam,* 31–32. Roy also mentions Shamil in the Caucasus, Mullah-i Lang in Afghanistan, the *akhund* of Swat in India, and 'Abd al-Karim in Morocco as representatives of this peripheral Sufi-led Islamic renewal and resistance to imperialism.

CHAPTER 3

[38]Mawdudi, *Let Us be Muslims,* 61–62; see also Mawdudi, *Towards Understanding Islam,* 62–65.

[39]*Kalima*—the Word (of God) is used in reference to the Quran.

[40]Mawdudi, *Let Us be Muslims,* 66.

[41]Qutb, *In the Shade of the Qur'an,* 119, 188, 241.

[42]Nadwi, *Muslims in the West,* 45–46. Abul Hasan 'Ali Nadwi (1914–1999) was one of the greatest fundamentalist Muslim scholars of our time.

[43]Ibrahim, et-al., *In Pursuit of Allah's Pleasure,* 30.

[44]Qutb, *In the Shade of the Qur'an,* 119, 188, 241.

[45]Murad, *Key to al-Baqarah,* 13–15. Khurram Murad (1932–1996) was a highly respected scholar and main leader in the Jama'at–i Islami.

[46]Qutb, *Milestones,* 11–13, 19.

[47]Ibid., 7, 15–16.

[48]Mawdudi, *Let Us be Muslims,* 45, 62–65.

[49]Ahmad, Khurshid, *Islam: Its Meaning and Message,* 31–32; 42–43; Khurshid Ahmad (1932) is a prominent economist, intellectual and scholar, former Vice-President of the *Jama'at-i Islami.*

[50]Shepard, "'Fundamentalism' Christian and Islamic," 362–363.

[51]Murad, *Way to the Qur'an*, 10–12, 25–35.

[52]Qutb, *Milestones*, 13–14, 30–33.

[53]Ibid., 13–14.

[54]Ahmad, "The Obligations Muslims Owe to the Qur'an": Israr Ahmad (1932–) is commander (*amir*) of the Pakistani *Tanzeem-e-Islami* movement.

[55]Qutb, *Sayyid Qutb and Islamic Activism,* 9–12, 278–279, 307.

[56]Ahmad, Israr, *Islam: Its Meaning and Message*, 34.

[57]Qutb, *In the Shade of the Qur'an*, 302.

[58]Ibid.

[59]al-Mas'ari, "Ruling by Kufr is Haram."

[60]Ibid.

[61]Abdelnasser, *The Islamic Movement in Egypt*, 197.

[62]Jihad—the struggle in God's way in all areas of life, including Holy War.

[63]Faraj, *The Neglected Duty,*166–175.

[64]Khomeini, *Light Within Me*, 121–123.

[65]Shariati, *On The Sociology of Islam*, 72; Shariati, *Man and Islam*, 2; Shariati, *What Is to Be Done*, 67–77.

[66]Zebiri, "Muslim Anti-Secularist Discourse in the Context of Muslim-Christian Relations," 52–53.

[67]Al-Banna, *Five tracts of Hasan al-Banna,*15–17, 89.

[68]Qutb, *Sayyid Qutb and Islamic Activism,* 298.

[69]Qutb, *Milestones*, 30, 67–69, 107–108; Nettler, "A Modern Confession of Faith and Conception of Religion," 102–114.

CHAPTER 4

[70]From 2 Corinthians 6:17.

[71]Qutb, *Milestones*, 14–16.

[72] Ibid., 113–114, 120.

[73]Jabbour, *The Rumbling Volcano*, 143–157; also Kepel, *The Prophet and The Pharaoh*, 95–96, 150.
[74]Dekmejian, *Islam In Revolution*, 92–96, 101.

CHAPTER 5
[75]From Isaiah 33:22.
[76]Qutb, *Milestones*, 25–27; Qutb, *Sayyid Qutb and Islamic Activism*, 26–29.
[77]Nettler, "A Modern Islamic Confession of Faith and Conception of Religion."
[78]Nadwi, *Muslims in the West*, 31.
[79]Ibid., 94–95.
[80]Ahmad, *Islam: Its Meaning and Message,* 29–31.
[81]Khamenei, *Essence of Tawhid*, 9–13, 24–25.
[82]Mawdudi, *The Islamic Movements*, 113–114.
[83]Mawdudi, *The Islamic Way of Life*, 9–10; Mawdudi, *Towards Understanding Islam*, 10, 18; Mawdudi, *Let Us be Muslims*, 79–81.
[84]Qutb, *Sayyid Qutb and Islamic Activism*, 8.
[85]Qutb, *Milestones*, 19–22.
[86]Ibid., 278–281.
[87]Ibid., 14–15; Mawdudi, *The Islamic Movement*, 30–32.
[88]Mawdudi, *The Islamic Movement*, 31–32.
[89]Shariati, *On the Sociology of Islam*, 82–83.
[90]Khamenei, *Essence of Tawhid*, 18–19.
[91]Ibid., 24–25.
[92]Ibid., 9–13, 24–25.

CHAPTER 6
[93]From Matthew 6:10.
[94]Lambton, *Islamic Fundamentalism*, 36–37, 46–47.
[95]Ibid., 278–281.

[96]al-Banna, *Five Tracts of Hasan al-Banna,* 24, 71–72.

[97]Mawdudi, *The Islamic State,* 23.

[98]Qutb, *Milestones,* 113, 120.

[99]Qutb, *Sayyid Qutb and Islamic Activism,* 277.

[100]Qutb, *Milestones,* 114, 120.

[101]"Declaration of The Conference of Islamic Revivalist Movements," Friday, November 20, 1998.

[102]Jama'at creed, *Azzam Publications.*

CHAPTER 7

[103]Romans 1:22.

[104]Qutb, *Milestones,* 11–113.

[105]Strawson, "Encountering Islamic Law," 11.

[106]Qutb, *Milestones,* 5–10, 15–17, 45–50, 66–67, 101, 123.

[107]Ibid., 64–68, 91–92.

[108]Strawson, "Encountering Islamic Law," 11.

[109]Jabbour, *The Rumbling Volcano,* 194–212; See also Abdelnasser, *The Islamic Movement in Egypt,* 204–205.

[110]Dekmejian, *Islam in Revolution,* 92–96.

[111]Faraj, *The Neglected Duty,* 169–175; See also Kepel, *The Prophet And The Pharaoh,* 191–222; Also Esposito, *The Islamic Threat: Myth Or Reality?,* 134–135.

CHAPTER 8

[112]Psalm 149:6–7a.

[113]Juergensmeyer, *The New Cold War?,* 156–160.

[114]Qutb, *Milestones,* 43–50.

[115]Mawdudi, *Jihad fi Sabilillah (Jihad in Islam),* 4–6, 10–11.

[116]Jabbour, *The Rumbling Volcano,* 194–212; See also Abdelnasser, *The Islamic Movement In Egypt,* 11, 197, 204–205.

[117]Faraj, *The Neglected Duty,* 159–179, 186–189, 192–193,

207–213; See also Ansari, "The Islamic Militants in Egyptian Politics," 136–137; also Esposito, *The Islamic Threat: Myth or Reality?,* 134–135.

[118]*Da'wa* is the missionary call to all people to submit to Islam, while *hisba* entails all the practical means of commanding the right and forbidding the wrong in society.

[119]Ibrahim, et-al., *In Pursuit of Allah's Pleasure,* 48–51, 76–77, 115, 123.

[120]Shariati, *Man and Islam*, 68, 75, 83; Shariati, *What is to be Done*, 1, 52–54; Shariati, *On the Sociology of Islam*, 39–42, 59–60; Shariati, *Martyrdom: Arise and Bear Witness*, 78.

[121]Ende and Steinbach, *Der Islam in der Gegenwart*, 96–98.

[122]al-Yasini, *Religion and State in the Kingdom of Saudi Arabia*, 28–29.

[123]Kostiner, "State, Islam and Opposition in Saudi Arabia," 75–89. Kostiner characterizes some opposition figures as Wahabbis who are modern-educated and influenced by ideas of the Muslim Brotherhood and radical revivalist groups in Egypt (81).

[124]On the rise of the Taliban, and on whether they are traditionalists or fundamentalists, see Maley, *Fundamentalism Reborn?*, 1–28.

[125]'Azzam, *Defense of the Muslim Lands,* 4–6.

[126]'Azzam, *Join the Caravan*, 36–38.

[127]'Azzam, *Defense of the Muslim Lands,* 7–17.

[128]Ibid., 29–33.

[129]"Conversation with Terror," Interview with Usama bin-Laden in *TIME*, January 11,1999, 34–35. See also "Terror Suspect," an ABC News interview with Usama bin-Laden conducted by Rahimullah Yousafsai in December, 1998.

[130]bin-Laden, "Declaration of War Against the Americans

Occupying the Land of the Two Holy Places." Qutb, *Milestones*, 94–96.

[131]Differences were based on confessional Sunni-Shia lines, on ethnic and tribal rivalries as well as on ideological nuances and on the backing of outside Muslim powers such as Pakistan, Iran, and Saudi-Arabia.

[132]Engel, "Inside Al-Qaeda: A Window into the World of Militant Islam and the Afghani Alumni;" See also Reeves, *The New Jackals*, 172–189; Also Shay and Schweitzer, "The 'Afghan Alumni' Terrorism."

[133]Reeves, *The New Jackals*, 232, on the radical groups establishing themselves in the United States.

[134]Rashwan, "A War over Resources." Rashwan makes a clear distinction between Islamist groups like *Jihad* and *al-Jamaa al-Islamiyya*, who espouse internal jihad against their own Muslim regimes towards creating Islamic states, and groups like *al-Qa'ida* who espouse external jihad against non-Muslim enemies. Of course the co-operation between the various groups in the Afghan war has led to a shift of the first in the direction of the second.

CHAPTER 9

[135]From Judges 16:30.

[136]bin-Laden, "Declaration of War Against the Americans Occupying the Land of the Two Holy Places."

[137]*Qa'idat al-jihad,* quoted by Reuven Paz.

[138]bin-Laden, "Declaration of War Against the Americans Occupying the Land of the Two Holy Places."

[139]Sardar, "Clinton Provokes a Jihad: Bin Laden vs. Hasan-e Sabah."

[140]Shariati, *Martyrdom*, 12, 50–51, 70–76, 89–91, 94.

[141]Roy, *The Failure of Political Islam,* 65–67; See also: Ben-

Dor, *Islamic Radicalism in the Greater Middle East,* 246–247.

[142]Harb, "The Truth about Martyrdom in Arab and Islamic Culture."

[143]Mneimneh and Makiya, "Manual for a Raid."

[144]Ibid.

[145]Shariati, *Martyrdom,* 12, 50–51, 70–76, 89–91, 94.

[146]Rubin, *Anti-American Terrorism and the Middle East*, 29.

[147]Ibid., 32–34.

[148]On the discussions between *'ulama'* on the question of suicide bombings in the context of the Palestinian uprising, see Yotam Feldner, "Debating the Religious, Political and Moral Legitimacy of Suicide Bombings."

[149]Abu Ruqaiyah, "The Islamic Legitimacy of the 'Martyrdom Operations'."

[150]Feldner, "Debating the Religious, Political and Moral Legitimacy of Suicide Bombings."

[151]Ibid.

[152]Article 6, *Ain-al-Yaqeen.*

[153]Chief Mufti of the Palestinian Police, Sheikh Abd al-Salam Abu Shukheydem, <http://www.memri.org/ia/lA7401.html>. See also <http://www.smh.com.au/news/0109/25/world/world106.html>.

[154]Harb, "The Truth About Martyrdom in Arab and Islamic Culture."

CHAPTER 10

[155]From 2 Peter 3:12.

[156]While the *dajjal* is not mentioned in the Quran, he has a prominent place in the Hadith collections.

[157]Sultan Firuz Shah of Delhi (d.1388) claimed that he executed those who claimed to be the *mahdi*, but only

imprisoned those who claimed to be God. *The Oxford Encyclopedia of Modern Islamic World*, Vol. 2., 27.

[158]Rapoport, *Fundamentalisms and the State,* 447, 450.

[159]Ibrahim, et-al., *In Pursuit of Allah's Pleasure,* 30–31. The authors, who are close to the Egyptian al-Jihad movement, include in their declaration of faith (*aqeedah*) the following items: "We have no doubt that the awaited Mahdee (or rightly-guided Imam) will come forth from among the *Ummah* of the Prophet at the end of time (on earth). We believe in the Signs of the Hour. The appearance of ad-Dajjal (false Messiah, or Antichrist). The descent from heaven of Isa, son of Mary. The sun rising from the West. The emergence of the Beast from the earth. And other signs mentioned in the Quran and the authentic Hadeeth of the Prophet."

[160]Faraj, *The Neglected Duty*, 163–164. See also Abdelnasser, *The Islamic Movement in Egypt,* 234–235.

[161]Rapoport, *Fundamentalisms and the State,* 447, 450.

[162]Abdelnasser, *The Islamic Movement in Egypt,* 216; See also Hopwood, *Egypt: Politics and Society 1945–1990,* 118.

[163]Al-Yassini, *Religion and State in the Kingdom of Saudi Arabia,* 124–129; Jahaymin (Juhayman) and his followers seized the Grand Mosque in 1979 and had to be dislodged by the security forces in a violent siege.

[164]Shariati, *Islam in Transition: Muslim Perspectives,* 298–304; See also Shariati, *On the Sociology of Islam,* 124.

[165]Dawoud, "America's Most Wanted." Dawoud states that "For his followers, bin-Laden is not just a political figure, but has a status almost akin to that of a saint or a messiah." He describes bin-Laden's ascetic lifestyle living in harsh surroundings in the mountains and caves of Afghanistan and surviving on a simple diet of cheese, milk and dates.

See also Pipes, "Muslims Love Bin Laden."

CHAPTER 11

[166]From Isaiah 8:12.

[167]Abanes, *American Militias: Rebellion, Racism and Religion,* 210–211.

[168]Broderick, "The Lunatic Fringes"; See also "John Birch Society."

[169]Abshire, "Counter-Cultural Christianity: Militias!"

[170]Zebiri, "Muslim Anti-Secularist Discourse in the Context of Muslim-Christian Relations," 3.

[171]Qutb, *Milestones,* 94–96.

[172]Qutb, *Sayyid Qutb and Islamic Activism,* 284–288.

[173]Abdelnasser, *The Islamic Movement in Egypt,* 226, 240–244, 254.

[174]Khomeini, *Islam in Transition,* 314–315.

[175]Khamenei, "No Need for Iran-US Negotiations."

[176]In its gathering in London, February 23, 1998, which included Usama bin-Laden (*al-Qa'ida*), Ayman al-Zawahiri (*al-Jihad*), Abu-Yasir Taha (*al-Jama'a al-Islamiyya*), Mir Hamza (*Jaô'yatul Ulama-i Pakstan*), and Fazlur Rahman (*Jihad* Movement Bangladesh). See World Islamic Front Statement, "Jihad Against Jews and Crusaders." This *fatwa* was based on the Quranic verses: "And fight the pagans all together as they fight you all together," and "fight them until there is no more tumult or oppression, and there prevail justice and faith in God."

[177]"Usamah Bin-Laden, the Destruction of the Base," an Interview with Usama bin-Laden conducted by Jamal Isma'il and aired June 10, 1999.

[178]bin-Laden, "Declaration of War Against the Americans Occupying the Land of the Two Holy Places"; See also

"Terror Suspect," an ABC News interview with Usama bin-Laden conducted by Rahimullah Yousafsai in December 1998.

[179]Ibid.

[180]The Illuminati were an eighteenth century Bavarian secret society linked to Freemasonry and banned by the authorities. Conspiracy theories involving the Illuminati were revived in twentieth century America.

[181]Abanes, *American Militias*, 143–168; See also Macdonald. *The Turner Diaries,* 29, 34, 42, 64.

[182]Qutb, *Milestones,* 94–96.

[183]Nettler, *Past Trials and Present Tribulations*, Foreword, x.

[184]Ibid., 81.

[185]Ibid., 72.

[186]Ibid. Also Qutb, *Milestones*, 94–96.

[187]Qutb, *Sayyid Qutb and Islamic Activism*, 303.

[188]Nettler, *Past Trials and Present Tribulations*, 75–85.

[189]*Al-Bayan* homepage, <http://www.ummah.net.pk/albayan>.

[190]al-Haidar. "Sufi-vs-Salafi: The Pot Calls the Kettle Black."

[191]"Talking with Terror's Banker," an ABC News interview with Usama bin-Laden conducted by John Miller, May 28, 1998.

[192]"Conversation with Terror," Interview with Usama bin-Laden, *TIME,* January 11, 1999.

[193]"Talking with Terror's Banker," an ABCNews interview with Usama bin-Laden conducted by John Miller, May 28, 1998.

[194]Kramer, "The Salience of Islamic Anti-Semitism."

[195]"Ahmad Rami's Idealism," a *Pravda* interview with Ahmad Rami, *Radio Islam,* July 15, 1997.

[196]"Right On!" by Jessie, *Radio Islam*.

CHAPTER **12**

[197]Abrogation is an integral part of classical Muslim theology. It claims that more recent Quranic texts abrogate earlier ones on the same subject. This invariably leads to aggressive Medina texts abrogating more conciliatory but earlier Meccan texts. The commands to fight and kill the infidels and apostates belong to the later texts and are seen as valid until the end of the world.

[198]There is much argument on what constitutes a "moderate" Muslim. Most would agree that moderate Muslims are those who renounce the use of force in achieving religious aims, balance the violent passages in the Muslim scriptures by prioritizing the more conciliatory passages as having equal or even greater validity, and accept Western ideas of the separation of religion and state and the importance of democracy and the freedoms it guarantees.

[199]Larson, *Evangelical Missions Quarterly*, 440–441.

Other books available from...

Gabriel
Publishing

PO Box 1047
129 Mobilization Dr
Waynesboro, GA 30830

706-554-1594
1-8MORE-BOOKS
gabriel@omlit.om.org
www.gabriel-resources.com

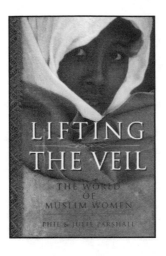

Lifting The Veil
The World Of Muslim Women

Phil and Julie Parshall

Secluded from the eyes of anyone but family members, Muslim women live under a system of tradition, rites and rituals that favor men above women. "A man loves first his son, then his camel, and then his wife," says an Arab proverb.

Phil and Julie Parshall understand the issues, heartaches and dangers facing Muslim women today, having lived among them for more than four decades. They bring a sensitive perspective to this thoughtful, yet sobering book that examines the controversy of female circumcision and proof of virginity, the heartache of arranged marriages, divorce, polygamy, and the status of women living in a male dominated world.

This book will not provide you with easy answers but will prompt you to begin praying for these "daughters of Ishmael," and give you sensitive awareness to life behind the veil.

1-884543-67-7   288 Pages

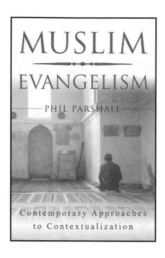

Muslim Evangelism
Contemporary Approaches To Contextualization
Revised Version of *New Paths In Muslim Evangelism*

Phil Parshall

It was this book which gave new, biblical meaning to the word "contextualization" and made that word the "hot topic" that it is in Muslim ministry today. If you want to understand deeply the issues at stake in Christian ministry among Muslims, then you must read this book.

Much has happened in our chaotic world since *New Paths In Muslim Evangelism* was first published in 1981. Muslims of the ultra-fundamentalist variety have terrorized millions. Westerners are perplexed. Are these "Followers of Muhammad" people of peace or are they religious fanatics bent on world domination?

In this important book, Phil Parshall seeks to acquaint the reader with the Muslim, not as a terrorist, but as one of the 1.3 billion who regard Islam as a "way of life" whose main concern is to provide for their families and to live in peace.

1-884543-79-0   304 Pages

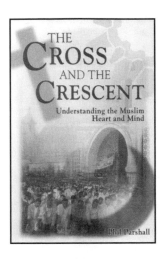

The Cross And The Crescent
Understanding The Muslim Heart And Mind

Phil Parshall

Who are the Muslims?

You hear about them in the news every day. Many people associate them with terrorism and cruelty. Some admire their willingness to die for their faith. Others wonder if there is more to Islam than fanaticism and martyrdom. And Christians ask, "How do we respond in faith and love to these people?" This question is more pressing than ever.

Phil Parshall understands the Muslim heart and mind. Living as a missionary among Muslims, he knows them - not as a band of fanatics on the evening news, but as individuals, some good, some bad. In this very warm, very personal book he looks at what Muslims believe and how their beliefs affect and often don't affect their behavior. He compares and contrasts Muslim and Christian views on the nature of God, sacred Scriptures, worship, sin and holiness, mysticism, Jesus and Muhammed, human suffering and the afterlife.

1-884543-68-5   320 Pages

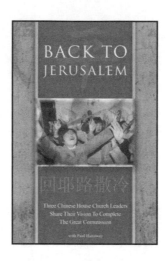

Back to Jerusalem

Three Chinese House Church Leaders Share Their Vision
to Complete the Great Commission

with Paul Hattaway

Napoleon once said: "When China is moved it will change the face of the globe." Today those words are becoming a reality through the powerful spiritual vision of the Chinese church to send 100,000 missionaries across China's borders to complete the Great Commission, even in this generation!

Here Brother Yun, Peter Xu Yongze and Enoch Wang, three Chinese house church leaders who between them have spent more than 40 years in prison for their faith, explain the history and present-day reality of the Back to Jerusalem movement. Christians everywhere who are called to fulfill the Great Commission, will be thrilled by this testimony and inspired to live bolder lives as disciples of Jesus Christ today.

1-884543-89-8   176 Pages

Cat and Dog Theology
Rethinking Our Relationship With Our Master

Bob Sjogren & Dr. Gerald Robison

There is a joke about cats and dogs that conveys their differences perfectly.

A dog says, "You pet me, you feed me, you shelter me, you love me, you must be God."
A cat says, "You pet me, you feed me, you shelter me, you love me, I must be God."

These God-given traits of cats ("You exist to serve me") and dogs ("I exist to serve you") are often similar to the theological attitudes we have in our view of God and our relationship to Him. Using the differences between cats and dogs in a light-handed manner, the authors compel us to challenge our thinking in deep and profound ways. As you are drawn toward God and the desire to reflect His glory in your life, you will worship, view missions, and pray in a whole new way. This life-changing book will give you a new perspective and vision for God as you delight in the God who delights in you.

1-884543-17-0   206 Pages